Meandering Pub Walks i

CW00842336

Chapters

1 Old Down: 2 miles: Fox Inn

2 Wanswell: 2.5 miles: Salmon Inn

3 Tytherington: 2.5 miles: The Swan

4 Oldbury on Severn: 3.5 miles: Anchor Inn

5 Littleton-upon-Severn: 3 miles: White Hart Inn

6 Rodborough: 2.5 miles: Bear of Rodborough Hotel

7 Berkeley/Ham: 5 miles: Salutation Inn

8 Uley: 3 miles: The Crown Inn

9 Purton via Brookend: 3.5 miles: Lammastide Inn Brookend

10 Upper Framilode; 2 miles Ship Inn.

DISCLAIMER

The contents of the book are correct at time of publication. However we cannot be held responsible for any errors or omissions or changes in details or for any consequences of any reliance on the information provided. We have tried to be accurate in the book, but things can change and would be grateful if readers advise me of any inaccuracies they may encounter.

I have taken every care to ensure the walks are safe and achievable by walkers with a reasonable level of fitness. But with outdoor activities there is always a degree of risk involved and the publisher accepts no responsibility for any injury caused to readers while following these walks.

SAFETY FIRST

All the walks have been covered to ensure minimum risk to walkers that follow the routes.

Always be particularly careful if crossing main roads, but remember traffic can also be dangerous even on minor country lanes.

If in the country and around farms be careful of farm machinery and livestock (take care to put dog on lead) and observe the **Country Code**.

Also ensure you wear suitable clothing and footwear, I would advise wearing walking boots which protect from wet feet and add extra ankle support over uneven terrain.

There are a few rules that should be observed if walking alone advise somebody were you are walking and approximate time you will return. Allow plenty of time for the walk especially if it is further and or more difficult than you have walked before. Whatever the distance make sure you have enough daylight hours to complete the walk safely. When walking along a country road always walk on the right to face oncoming traffic, the only exception is on a blind bend were you cross to the left to have a clear view and can be seen from both directions.

If bad weather should come in making visibility difficult, do not panic just try to remember any features along route and get out the map to pinpoint the area but be sure before you move off, that you are moving in the right direction.

Unfortunately accidents can still happen even on the easiest of walks, if this is the case make sure the person in trouble is safe before seeking help. If carrying a mobile phone dial 999 or 112 European Union emergency number will connect you to any network to get you help.

Unmapped walks we recommend that you take the relevant Ordnance Survey map and compass with you, even if you have a Smartphone, digi-walker or G.P.S all of which can fail on route.

Introduction

This book contains ten easy to follow walks with clear instructions as to access where to start, type of pub and opening times, all the walks are circular and they range in distances from 2 miles to 5 miles depending on how far you want to walk. There is also a walk time but this is just a guide to estimate if you can do the walk before closing time?

Please whenever you are out and about make sure you follow the Countryside Code, gates are normally shut by the farmers to keep farm animals in, sometimes they may be left open so animals can reach food or water. So be sure to leave gates as you find them or follow instructions on any signs on the gate.

Please remember all walks may have an element of danger whether it is cattle that might want to chase you or extremely high tides, potholes or may be uneven ground. So always wear walking boots that will give support over poor terrain by binding and protecting the ankles or help stop wet feet to safe guard from blisters. Before setting out try to eliminate any problems and remember you might want to pack good waterproof clothing and may be a change of clothes in the car, do not forget the water.

Also on the book list is the O.S map for the area the walk is in this is always a good idea to take may be as a back for G.P.S. or Smartphone all of which can fail or not work in some areas. The O.S maps are also very detailed and can point troubles that can occur along the way and also include in the kit a compass never fails unlike technology.

In most of the pubs well behaved dogs are also welcome if not inside then usually there is a nice beer garden and a bowl of cool water. Please remember if it is extremely hot then make sure you have plenty of water and the dog to avoid dehydration.

The walks are all varied and some can be done through all the seasons due to walking of country lanes, but bear in mind that some walks the paths may be extremely wet or flooded or they might just be bogged down with thick mud, also remember to check before leaving home that the pub near where you are going is open in the winter to avoid disappointment.

WARNING
Ticks can be a problem at certain times of the year, they can give you Lym Disease a bacterial infection that can be passed to humans through this small blood sucking insect. Ticks can be found commonly in woodland, grassland and heathland either in the U.K. or abroad. To check symptoms go to the website of Natural England.
Happy Walking.

Meandering Pub Walks in Gloucestershire.

Chapter 1 Old Down: Fox Inn;

Park & Start Grid ref; ST 610866

Distance: 2 Miles

Level: Easy

Time: 1 hour 30 minutes

Terrain: Country lanes open fields and through wooded area paths.

Maps. O.S Explorer 167 Thornbury, Dursley and Yate.

Refreshments: Fox Inn.

The Fox Inn.

The Old down Woods.

The Pub; BS35 4PR

This pub is certainly of the beaten track, which uses walkers for a passing trade along with the locals. On approaching the Fox Inn you encounter the back first which is not very inviting but around the corner there is a nice frontage with a green and picnic tables for those sunny days. It is a very welcome sight for the walkers with the addition of good food and ale.

Opening Times;

Monday to Saturday 11.30 am to 11.00 pm Sunday 11.00 am to 11.00 pm

Access to start;

Leave M5 motorway at junction 16 on the slip road to Filton/Thornbury and then at the roundabout go off at 3rd exit onto the A38/Gloucester Road. Continue on the A38 for about 1.5 miles and then turn left onto Fernhill. Then after a half mile turn right onto Lower Tockington Road, then bear to the right and then to the left onto Washingpool Hill Road where you can find somewhere to park.

The Walk

(1)

The walk starts off in Tockington, where you can park anywhere on Washingpool Hill Road near to Manor Park. Stay on road and follow through the village go past the Tockington Manor School on the left opposite the beautiful Pavilion building and then follow from the last of the school buildings the wall along the edge of the road. Follow the wall to its end, where it turns left onto a driveway after about half a mile.

(2)

Turn left onto the driveway which is marked public footpath and then follow it on up to the large house straight ahead. Keep over to the left at the house and follow the well-defined path around the outside of the house to a public footpath sign pointing up the field in the direction of the woods. Follow the path up the field and enter Old down Woods via a concealed entrance and then stay close to the fence on the right to follow the path uphill to reach a stile at the top.

(3)

Cross the stile and follow the path straight ahead up through the field to reach a small gate in the corner that goes out through the narrow path between houses to finally emerge on the lane named The Down in the hamlet of Old Down. Then from here to go to The Fox Inn turn right and after just a few metres turn right again down a lane called The Inner Down to locate The Fox Inn in on the right. Then to continue the walk from the pub retrace your steps back to The Down follow on straight ahead to reach a road junction after about 25 metres onto Alveston Road.

(4)

Turn left on the Alveston Road and then carefully cross road to pavement and then walk for about half a mile to reach a crossroads. At the crossroads on the right is Foxholes Road, but for us cross road and walk down on the left Old Down Hill with sign post marked Tockington. Continue to follow lane downhill with no pavement for the first 400 metres, you then can walk down on the grass verge. When you get midway downhill and right on the bend for safety conditions take the path up a few steps along the edge of the woods, this is just a short distance to exit wooded area then follow on down path to the end of Old Down Hill to reach a road junction. At the road junction of Washingpool Hill Road you turn left or right depending on where you parked on the road in Tockington village.

Chapter 2 Wanswell: Salmon Inn;

Park & Start Grid ref; ST 683015

Distance: 2 Miles

Level: Easy

Time: 1 hour 30 minutes

Terrain: Country lanes open fields and through wooded area paths.

Maps. O.S Explorer 167 Thornbury, Dursley and Yate.

Refreshments: Salmon Inn.

The Salmon Inn.

Out in the Countryside

The Pub; GL13 9SE

This is a proper English pub set in a quaint village with no music or fruit machines just the right atmosphere for talking and relaxing. There is also a great outdoor space with a lawn area with picnic tables for the better weather. Then inside the pub the floor as been stripped which gives a nice contemporary space for meeting friends and enjoying the ambiance. The food and ale are very good, with things like Cotswold Venison, cheddar ploughman dish or a very nice fish pie. The menu is varied with all fresh and locally sourced.

Opening Times

Monday to Saturday 11.30 am to 11.00 pm Sunday 11.00 am to 11.00 pm

Access to start

Leave the M5 motorway at junction 14 and take slip road onto the B4509 towards Dursley. Then turn right onto the A38 and follow for just under 4 miles to turn left onto Alkington Lane. Then after about half a mile turn left onto the A4066 and then at roundabout take the 2nd exit. At the next roundabout take 3rd exit onto Station Road to park near the Salmon Inn.

The Walk

(1)

The walk starts off on Station Road so park near to the Salmon Inn. Then with the Salmon Inn on your right, walk down the road and just past the school take the first turning left on to a narrow lane. Then stay on the lane for about a half mile to the end to reach a farm down on the right.

(2)

Go past the farm buildings on right, and be sure to keep well over to the left to walk along a muddy pathway section by a hedge in front of the farm house on the right. Continue down the edge of a tree line to reach a gate straight ahead. Then go through gate turn left and follow the path through the field next to the hedge towards the end of the field. Just before the end on left go through a gap in hedge and follow the path diagonally to the left to reach a large metal gate at the end of the field.

(3)

Once through gate turn left onto Halmore Lane and follow the lane for just over half a mile back into Wanswell village. Then at the road junction with Station Road turn left or right depending on where you parked or if you are then going into the Salmon Inn.

Chapter 3 Tytherington: Swan Inn;

Park & Start Grid ref; ST 669882

Distance: 2.5 Miles

Level: Easy

Time: 1 hour 30 minutes

Terrain: Country lanes open fields and through green lanes.

Maps. O.S Explorer 167 Thornbury, Dursley and Yate.

Refreshments: Swan Inn.

The Swan Inn.

The merging of Green Lanes

The Pub; GL12 8QB

This is an elegant 16th century village pub which is well known for its quality cuisine. It as the old classic oak beams and inglenook fireplaces which help to create a wonderful country pub atmosphere. The food and ale is extremely good with an excellent selection on the menu for both lunch and evening meal.

Opening Times

Monday to Saturday 12.00 pm to 11.00 pm
Sunday 12.00 pm to 10.00 pm

Access to start
Leave the M5 motorway at junction 14 then take the slip road onto the B4509 towards Thornbury. Then leave the B4509 onto the A38, and after about 3 miles turn left onto Tytherington Road, this road changes name to Stowell Hill Road to arrive in Tytherington. Turn right just before The Swan Inn and then almost immediately turn right again onto West Street to park.

The Walk

(1)

The walk starts off from behind The Swan in the centre of the village of Tytherington. Take the lane to the right West Street and park on road. Then walk down West Street to the road junction at the bottom, turn right onto Itchington Road and follow road through the village, under the railway bridge then on out the village into the country. Stay on the lane for best part of a mile to reach a large white house on the right, then continue for a further 25 metres to reach a sharp left hand bend.

(2)

At the bend you will notice a signpost on right marked public footpath, turn right up green lane and continue to follow for over a mile to come into a farm. Walk straight through the farm yard with the farm house off to the left and on past farm buildings on the right to reach a narrow lane at the top of the small slope.

(3)

Once you have reached this point, you can take a slight detour by turning to the left. This will take you up the narrow lane for about half a mile to look out over the magnificent landscape in all directions. There was once an Old Fort up the hill near the top on the right but unfortunately that as gone it is now just a quarry site.

(4)

If however you just want to continue your walk then turn right at the top of the slope, you are now back on West Street so just follow the road down under a railway bridge to reach the parked car at the bottom of the street.

Chapter 4 Oldbury on Severn: Anchor Inn

Park & Start Grid ref; ST 608924

Distance: 3.5 Miles

Level: Easy

Time: 1 hour 45 minutes

Terrain: Country lanes open fields and through green lanes.

Maps. O.S Explorer 167 Thornbury, Dursley and Yate.

Refreshments: Anchor Inn.

The Anchor Inn.

Severn Way with Oldbury Power Station in the distance.

The Pub; BS35 1QA
This is a very good pub set in the beautiful area of Oldbury. The pub won the value pub of the year in 2013 with its well priced and good quality food. The dining room is light and airy with double doors out onto a magnificent garden, which also as a boules area at the bottom.

Opening Times
Monday to Friday 11.30am – 2.30pm, 6pm – 11.00pm
Saturday   **11.30am – 12.00 midnight**
Sunday   **12 noon – 10.30pm**

Access to start
Leave M5 motorway at junction 16 and take the slip road down to the traffic lights and then turn left to continue on through Almondsbury. Continue straight on to next traffic lights and turn left to Thornbury, take Grovesend Road and follow on through to Gloucester Road B4061 onto Butts Lane that changes to Oldbury Lane and follow signs into Oldbury-on-Severn.

The Walk

(1)

The walk starts near the Anchor Inn in the centre of the village, there is plenty of parking at the side of the road or the car park for the pub overflow. Take the narrow lane next to the overflow car park signposted to the Sailing Club which is also part of the Severn Way and follow down to the River Severn.

(2)

Once at the River Severn keep to the right and follow for about a mile making sure you take in the spectacular views out over the River Severn to the Forest of Dean and looking back to Bristol with the clear view of the magnificent Severn Bridge. Then continue on with the view of the Oldbury Nuclear Power Station getting ever closer, this of course as now been decommissioned. Then on approaching the Power Station turn right down a track that runs parallel with the Power Station next to the perimeter fence, which after about 500 metres reaches a road. Turn right on the road and then continue to follow for another half mile ignoring various turnings, to reach along the road a clump of trees on the right with a narrow track at the end of the trees.

(3)

Turn right down the track which is Ham Lane a very old green lane, this sweeps across many entrances to fields which makes it easy to enter fields for farming purposes. Continue the walk down Ham Lane which brings you to the outskirts of Oldbury-on-Severn. Just ignore several turnings off Ham Lane to continue on to enter Camp Road which is after about a mile. Then stay on Camp Road which at the end comes to a crossroads with Featherbed Lane and Chapel Road. At this point go straight ahead onto Church Lane and then just retrace your steps back to the parked car.

(4)

Once in Church Lane you might like a tea or coffee at the nice little Community Shop and café on the right just before the Anchor Inn.

Chapter 5 Littleton on Severn: White Hart Inn;

Park & Start Grid ref; ST 595899

Distance: 3 Miles

Level: Easy

Time: 1 hour 30 minutes

Terrain: Country lanes open fields and through green lanes.

Maps. O.S Explorer 167 Thornbury, Dursley and Yate.

Refreshments: White Hart Inn.

The White Hart Inn.

The Severn Bridge in the distance.

The Pub; BS35 1NR
This a beautiful country pub set in an original 17th century Farmhouse which gives it its charm and elegance. Large garden front and back with an orchard also at the back. The food and the ale is of very high standard and quality in all a well-hidden gem.

Opening Times
Open daily from 12 noon but food served at a set time only, check website.

Access to start
Leave M5 motorway at junction 16 and take the slip road down to the traffic lights and then turn left to continue on through Almondsbury. Continue straight on to next traffic lights and turn left to Thornbury, take Grovesend Road and follow on through to Gloucester Road B4061, turn on to Park Road, and then a left onto Castle Street, take another right onto Kington Lane and follow through to Stoke Hill then follow signs into Littleton upon Severn.

The Walk

(1)

The walk starts on Church Road near to the White Hart Public House, walk up the village to the Littleton Church on the left and then turn right directly opposite down Rushen Lane signposted bridleway and to Severn Way. Once on the lane and after about 100 metres you will come to a fork in the lane, take the left lane and then just continue to walk for about a mile looking at the views and a quick glimpse of the Severn Bridge on the left. Just stay on Rushen Lane to the end with the track going off to the right but go straight ahead to a large metal gate.

(2)

Go through the metal gate and into a field, then follow the pathway down through the first field through a gateway into another field. Stay on the track down the field keeping the hedge on your right, then towards the bottom of the field head away from the bottom right hand side of the field to head for a small kissing gate set in the hedge.

(3)

Go through the kissing gate and climb up the bank onto the Severn Way. Then stay on the Severn Way for just under a half mile to reach a small inlet on the left, at this point take the path off to the right through a gate which leads out onto the lane at Whale Wharf.

(4)

Having reached the lane turn right and follow this quiet country lane for about 1.25 miles making sure you take in the beautiful views out over the fields and down to the River Severn. Just continue past a row of cottages on right to reach a triangular shaped green with trees, then turn right onto the lane and follow for a short distance back into the village, then retrace your final steps back to the car via the White Hart Inn.

Chapter 6 Rodborough: Bear of Rodborough;

Park & Start Grid ref; SO 851040

Distance: 2.5 Miles

Level: Easy

Time: 1 hour 30 minutes

Terrain: Country lanes, open fields, woodland, common and through green lanes.

Maps. O.S Explorer 168 Stroud, Tetbury and Malmesbury.

Refreshments: White Hart Inn.

Bear of Rodborough.

High up near Rodborough Common.

The Pub; GL5 5DE
This is a place of real atmosphere The Bear Bar and Common room are comfortable with a nice open log fire for the winter. There is also a nice garden area to sit in the summer months.

Opening Times Bar
Drinks 10.00am to late
Lunch 12.00 noon to 3,00pm
Dinner 6.30pm to 9.30pm

Access to start
Leave Stroud via A4171 Pagan Hill Lane, then at the roundabout take 2nd exit onto A419 Dudbridge Road. At next roundabout take 1st exit onto A46 Dudbridge Hill, then keep right and stay on A46 Dudbridge Road. After about 1.5 miles turn left onto Bear Hill and park midway uphill off a sharp bend, entrance on left over a cattle grid.

The Walk

(1)

The walk starts at the National Trust car park halfway up Bear Hill off to the left. Exit the car park in the direction of the road, then very carefully cross the road and straight ahead, then almost immediately with a large white gate in front turn left and follow a narrow path next to a wall. After just a short distance you reach a wooden gate go through into the woods. Then stay on upper path and continue along what was the old pack horse trail on through the woods. The path then starts to sweep around to the right past what was once an old building on the right, then just keep following the path on through the woods to reach an archway which forms part of a bridge used for the pack horses.

(2)

Go up the slope and turn left across the old pack horse bridge above the archway and then climb on up a steep hill, then at the top follow the wall around to the right around the boundary of a house and continue on to turn left then finally reach the road at the top. Turn left out on the road and then continue to follow for about a half mile to reach the back of the Bear of Rodborough on the crossroads.

(3)

Cross over the road with extreme care near the Bear of Rodborough and then follow the path slightly to the left on a high plateau that further down opens into a wide space with magnificent views out over Woodcester and surrounding area. Then just before carry on down path along the ridge, turn off left down a narrow path that descends rapidly downhill. Keep dropping downhill towards the woodland which will then bring you out in the woods next to the layby where you parked the car.

Chapter 7 Ham: Salutation Inn

Park & Start Grid ref; ST 679983

Distance: 5 Miles

Level: Easy

Time: 2 hour

Terrain: Country lanes, open fields and Severn Way.

Maps. O.S Explorer 167 Thornbury, Dursley and Yate.

Refreshments: Salutation Inn.

The Salutation Inn.

The view from the Severn Way.

The Pub; GL13 9QH
The Sally is a multi-award winning pub including the National Pub of the Year 2014, the snacks and ale are very good. But the website puts it into perspective and that is you'll just have to come and see for yourselves.

Opening Times
Monday 5pm to 11.00pm
Tuesday to Friday 12 noon to 2.30pm and 5pm to 11pm
Saturday 12 noon to 11.00pm
Sunday 12 noon to 10.30pm

Access to start
Leave Berkeley via Marybrook Street and on towards Lower Berrycroft the road then changes name to Market Place. Turn right onto the High Street and keep straight on into Ham, then park on road near the Salutation Inn.

The Walk

(1)

The walk starts off parking along the road near to the Salutation Inn. Then walk out of Ham away from the direction of Berkeley and turn right at a road junction with a small triangular grass area set in the middle of the road junction on the right. Then once you are on the lane check out the Deer Park up to the left this runs parallel with the road for quiet away along the 1.5 miles, ignore tracks and lanes along the way to finally reach a crossroads. At the crossroads on either side there are no through road with a farm entrance on the left. But for the walk turn right at this point and follow Severn Lane for about another mile to reach a farm straight ahead, then follow the sign Severn Way to the right which directs you to a gate, go through gate and then up the bank to the Severn Way.

(2)

The views up on the Severn Way are quiet spectacular high up on the bank looking across to the Forest of Dean and down towards Bristol. Turn right on this first section of the Severn Way which is a nice concrete path, then you leave via a gate on to the next section which is a bit uneven and usually as livestock in the field. This is the section where you move away from the River Severn to follow the narrow path that then twist and turns around the outer perimeter of Berkeley Power Station. It continues on for quiet away through the countryside for about a mile to finally reach the road near the entrance to Berkeley Power Station.

(3)

Turn right on the road and then follow back for about half a mile before taking the first turning right onto Hamfield Lane. Then once on Hamfield Lane just settle back into an even pace soak up the views for about 1.5 miles to the end of the road at a junction. Then with the Salutation Inn (The Sally) directly ahead is it refreshments? Or back to the car depending on where on the road you parked.

Chapter 8 Uley: Old Crown Inn

Park & Start Grid ref; ST 789984

Distance: 2.5 Miles

Level: Easy

Time: 1 hour 45 minutes

Terrain: Country lanes, open fields and Millennium Green.

Maps. O.S Explorer 167 Thornbury, Dursley and Yate.

Refreshments: Old Crown Inn.

The Old Crown Inn.

View out over the country towards Owlpen Manor.

The Pub; GL11 5SN
This is a magnificent 17th century Coaching Inn on the edge of the Cotswolds in the village of Uley. The ales are good with some being brewed at the nearby Uley Brewery, the food is great all home cooked using local produce were possible.

Opening Times
Monday to Saturday 12.00 noon to 11.00pm
Sunday 12.00 noon to 22.30pm

Access to Start
Leave the A38 in direction of sign to Dursley, then follow the A4135 out of Dursley this then changes to B4066 which leads directly into Uley. Park on the road in the High Street.

The Walk

(1)

The walk starts in the centre of the village of Uley where you can park on the main road which is called The Street. Once you have parked up then slowly walk up the hill and on past St Giles Church on the left, then after about 50 metres you reach The Old Crown Inn on the corner of The Street and Fiery Lane. Turn right down Fiery Lane in the direction of Owlpen Manor, then continue along lane for what must be almost 2 miles (it seemed more) taking in the breath taking views which get better the higher you rise uphill, this is I am afraid a very long and hard climb to finally reach the top of the hill.

(2)

Toward the end of the climb there is a farm on the left and then after about 25 metres you reach a road junction. Turn right at junction and take care of cars as the road drops downhill and around some sharp bends, then midway down you go under a canopy of trees with woodland on both sides of the road which then opens out as you start to come into the outskirts of Uley village.

(3)

Then just before you reach the houses and with the start of a golf course on the left, turn right to crossover a stile marked with a public footpath sign which points you in the right direction across the field. The exit is across the field and then at the bottom of a slope with a small pathway through the hedge go over a bridge across a stream which then leads up into the Millennium Green, this is a very beautiful area set up for walkers and locals to enjoy the tranquil surroundings.

(4)

To continue the walk follow the well-defined path up the slope and out the exit area through a narrow path to come out on a cul-de-sac, then just off to the right is a café tucked away in the corner. But to continue the walk just follow the road for about 30 metres to road junction onto The Street then from here just navigate back to the parked car.

Chapter 9 Purton: Lammastide Inn Brookend

Park & Start Grid ref; SO 691044

Distance: 4 Miles

Level: Easy

Time: 1 hour 45 minutes

Terrain: Country lanes, Canal towpath.

Maps. O.S Explorer 167 Thornbury, Dursley and Yate.

Refreshments: Lammastide Inn Brookend.

Lammastide Inn Brookend.

Gloucester and Sharpness Canal at Purton.

The Pub; GL13 9SF
This is a warm and friendly pub with all welcome from walkers and even dogs, there are pictures in the bar area from the past on the walls which helps to make this a traditional country pub. The food and ale are good with a grand selection on the menu.

Opening Times
Monday to Friday 12.00 to 3.00pm and 6pm to 12 midnight
Saturday and Sunday 12.00 noon to 12.00 midnight

Access to start
LeaveA38 onto the road signposted to Purton, then turn right towards Riddle Street and keep on Riddle Street, then bear left to arrive in Purton. Cross Swing Bridge and park in layby near the Gloucester and Sharpness Canal.

The Walk

(1)

The walk starts from the layby near the swing bridge on the Gloucester and Sharpness Canal at Purton. Leave the layby and walk back over the swing bridge to reach a road junction after 50 metres. Turn right at junction on the lane to Hinton. Go past several houses along first section and look out to the right for brief glimpse of the River Severn in the distance. The lane then starts to rise uphill and then towards midway on the right is an open gateway that looks down towards the River Severn. Carry on along this long and winding road past a group of houses in Hinton until you come to the Malt House on the right this is about 1.5 miles from the beginning of the walk, at the next road junction about 50 metres on, then turn right onto the road to Sharpness (to go to the Lammastide Inn carry straight on into Brookend).

(2)

 To continue the walk after refreshment turn right and walk up the lane in the direction of Sharpness, then on past Lugg's Farm on the right but still heading for Sharpness then after about a half mile you reach a road junction. Do not turn left into Sharpness but go right down a no through road and continue to the end of the road with a large red brick house on the right, then follow the Severn Way marked signpost turning left down a slope to cross an old bridge. Then go on to cross another old decaying railway bridge to join a road at the end. Go straight ahead at this point and cross another bridge with views out over Sharpness Docks, then just carry on a short distance to the end of the road at a junction and turn right.

(3)

After turning right almost immediately turn right again and walk up a slight hill to the Vindicatrix Monument, then take the narrow track to the left of monument and continue straight ahead, this then takes you down to the Old Docks and the search and rescue boat area.

(4)

Continue to follow the path down and around the tidal basin and Old Harbour Masters house and then on to the start of the Sharpness Marina with its varied array of boats. Then continue through the marina on the tow-path to exit at a gate, then follow the Gloucester and Sharpness Canal tow-path taking in the views out over the River Severn and the old ship graveyard along the way, go past the two large pillars that once supported the Severn Railway Bridge that once spanned the River Severn. Then finally after about 1.5 miles you arrive back in Purton next to the layby by the swing bridge.

Chapter 10 Upper Framilode: Ship Inn

Park & Start Grid ref; SO 750104

Distance: 2 Miles

Level: Easy

Time: 1 hour 30 minutes

Terrain: Country lanes, Severn Way.

Maps. O.S Explorer 167 Thornbury, Dursley and Yate.

Refreshments: Ship Inn.

The Ship Inn.

River Severn near Upper Framilode.

The Pub; GL2 7LH

The Ship Inn is a well-positioned pub close to the River Severn and the nearby defunct Stroud Waterway Canal the pub has been here since 1779 when the canal was first opened. The Ship Inn serves good home cooked food with a very varied menu and good ale. The staff are very friendly there is a good atmosphere.

Opening Times

Daily 12.00 noon to 3.30pm and 6pm to 11pm.

Access to start

Leave A38 to turn off to Frampton on Severn, then leave on Whitminister Lane towards Oatfield Road. Turn right onto B4071 High Street, and then turn left to Upper Framilode.

The Walk

(1)

The walk starts off at a layby near St Peters Church and the River Severn. Park up and with the church on the left cross a stile up to the right and then follow the Severn Way along the riverbank. If however this is too wet or muddy then use the route by following the higher bank through the fields and over two stiles stay close to the hedge that also runs parallel with the River Severn. Continue on path to reach a gate, then go through the gate on into Lower Framilode, then follow lane past Framilode Mill and what was the Darrell Arms which is now a private residence. Then just stay on the lane to reach a road junction at the end.

(2)

Turn left at the road junction and carry on around the bend and then start to climb a slight uphill rise along Passage Road heading in the direction of Saul. Keep going on the road to reach a road junction with a bus shelter and a circular piece of grass with a signpost, and at junction continue to follow in the direction of Saul. Go past several houses on the left and right but continue on the lane for about another mile to reach another road junction.

(3)

At the road junction with Moor Lane turn left and walk for about half a mile past a built up area to a red brick bridge over what was the Stroud Waterway Canal. On the edge of the bridge area is a signpost marked public footpath (no horses) and if you turn left here and follow the tow-path along the Old Stroud Waterway Canal to the end, then at the lane turn left this will take you back to the layby.

(4)

If however to go on to the Ship Inn then stay on the road and continue for another 50 metres to see the Ship Inn sign at the edge of a driveway, turn left on drive to enter the pub area. Then when you are ready to leave exit driveway and turn left and again after about 50 metres turn left at a lane marked with a signpost saying public footpath Severn Way, and just follow lane back to the layby and the waiting car.

More Information on the Meandering Walking Series Paperbacks.

Meandering in Mid Devon
Meandering in South Devon
Meandering on Rivers and Canals in Devon
Meandering Pub Walks in Devon
Meandering Tea Rooms Walks in Devon
Meandering in Gloucestershire
Meandering on the Exe Estuary Trail
Meandering Through History, Mysteries or Legends in Devon
Meandering Pub Walks in Gloucestershire
Meandering with Man's Best Friend in Devon (January 2016)
Meandering the Severn Vale (March 2016)
Meandering More Pub Walks in Devon (later 2016)

Checkout some of the photos from the Meandering Walking Series

John coombes google plus

Website:

http://johncoombes.wix.com/meandering-walks-2

Remains of the Old Railway Bridge that spanned the River Severn.

Printed in Great Britain
by Amazon

First Class English Literature Essays

By Joanne M. Weselby

Licence Notes

Copyright: Joanne M. Weselby
Published: 27th August 2014
ISBN: 978-1500953904
CreateSpace Edition

Contents

From *Beowulf* to Blake: The Evolution of the Individual Identity
(An Exploration of Identity in *Beowulf*, *Hamlet* and *The Marriage of Heaven and Hell*)

Our understanding of the self and our individual identity has progressed spectacularly over the last five centuries or so. This development can be mapped through literature and art of the modern world, as well as by observing factual historical accounts. As our society has evolved, so have the heroes created by its members. The construction of their fictional identities is influenced by the thoughts and behaviour of their creators, who, in turn, have been shaped by the social structure they operate within. Therefore, a text could be considered as a record of the shared consciousness of a given time, its intertextuality revealing how members of a given society defined their identities.

An increasing societal awareness of the importance of the individual identity developed as a result of the European Renaissance in the fourteenth century, during which the artistic and literary emphasis shifted onto exploration of the uniqueness of each individual being. Before this realisation of self occurred, the importance of the needs of society overrode those of the individual. To be 'good' meant to adhere to ideals dictated by the ruling, moral power: the Church. The teachings of the Old Testament became a template for acceptable modes of behaviour and thoughts. People understood themselves in context of the value placed on them by others, the purpose that they served within their community and how their deeds would be judged after death.

Beowulf demonstrates this archaic approach to the portrayal of identity. It expresses the ideals of an ancient Germanic society but its morals are heavily influenced by the religion of its narrator. The text is rife with demonstrations of Christian ideals and morals, albeit disguised under the cloak of paganism. Judgements are passed by the narrator on the characters' religion ('sometimes at pagan shrines they vowed offerings to idols... the lord God... was unknown to them... [and so each has] thrust his soul in the fire's embrace'[1]). The construction of Beowulf's identity in this text is censored – he is only allowed to exhibit traits which adhere to the ideals of the society he represents. This restriction placed upon the exploration of identity mirrors societal expectations for all its citizens to become morally superior. In *Beowulf*, emphasis is placed on how he 'behaved with honour in battle'[2] (ln2178), showed kindness and was a 'wise... warden of the land'[3]: behavioural ideals that the Christian audience would be able to identify with. Despite the blood he has shed, he is portrayed as being without sin: whiter than white, a saviour to his people. The biblical connotations of this 'saviour' identity make the source of inspiration easily identifiable – even his chosen enemies are '[the] outcasts of God'[4]. However, this is

[1] S. Heaney, *Beowulf* (bilingual edition), (London: Faber and Faber, 2007) lns175-185
[2] *Beowulf* (bilingual edition), ln2178
[3] *Beowulf* (bilingual edition), lns2209-2210

juxtaposed alongside the idea of a blood-drenched, 'heathenish' pagan that '[remembers] hell'[5] without irony or apology. The definition of identity is limited and primitive.

A revolution in humanist thinking, combined with a deviation from the enforcement of biblical ideals, allowed artists to explore the individual identity with more freedom and honesty than ever before. The literature produced during this period became more explorative and intrinsic. During the sixteenth century, the movement's influence reached England. The progression it caused is evident in *Hamlet;* it demonstrates sharper definitions of individual and societal roles and of public and private identities. Understandably then, *Hamlet* offers the audience a very different kind of prince to *Beowulf;* his identity provides a near-polar opposition to the ancient warrior's. Although the heroes' societal positions may be similar (Hamlet is the heir to the throne of Denmark and Beowulf is crowned King of the Geats), Beowulf's representation in the text only addresses his societal role. Hamlet's complex character cannot be defined so simplistically. The text itself is famous for its multiple personality, split between Quarto and Folio (noted by Dillon[6]). *Hamlet* has been re-interpreted so often, many believe that it has lost touch with its original self[7]. Croxford believes this confusion is due

---

[4] *Beowulf* (bilingual edition), lns106-107
[5] *Beowulf* (bilingual edition), lns179-180
[6] J. Dillon, 'Is There A Performance In This Text?', *Shakespeare Quarterly*, 45 (1994), pp.74-87
[7] Rob Pope, 'The Not-So-Strange Case of Shakespeare's Hamlet', in *The English Studies Book: An Introduction to Language, Literature and Culture* (second edition) (Oxon: Routledge, 2002) pp.78-81

to 'the dramatist's need to integrate [both] his medieval and Renaissance sources'[8], even though definitions of identity in these two periods contradict one another. Shakespeare allows for the development of a pluralistic identity in the text, full of conflicts and oppositions. This demonstrates an evolutionary leap forward in the understanding of the human identity and the possibilities it holds for intricacy and paradoxical desires. Hamlet exhibits a fully-formed, interior self in this text alongside his public persona: something previously unheard of. A division in his personality is created, separating his position within society (a prince) from his individual self (a grieving son of a murdered father). Hamlet's *real*, authentic self is a socially unknown, protected being, free from the demands of the public group. However, this private self is at war with its counterpart for much of the play as they compete for domination of the protagonist's will, disrupting one another. Hamlet tries to hide his own way of *being* (his personal self) to *seem* unsuspicious to others. This implies that *seeming* is the exterior lie and *being* is the interior truth (alluded to almost immediately in the text: '*seems*, madam? … nay it *is*, I know not *seems*'[9]). He must honour his true self and obey its wishes to avenge his father. However, he cannot publicly declare his intentions or acknowledge his ghostly motivator: he must continue with his charade of normality whilst employing

---

[8] L. Croxford, 'The Uses of Interpretation in Hamlet', *Alif: Journal of Comparative Poetics*, 24 (2004), pp.93-120
[9] W. Shakespeare, *Hamlet* in *William Shakespeare: The Complete Works* (second edition), ed. by Stanley Wells and Gary Taylor (Oxford: Oxford University Press, 2005), Act I, Scene II, lns76-86

subtler methods to determine whether the ghost is an '[honest] spirit... or goblin damned'[10]. He must convince himself fully of the truth before taking action (resulting in Hamlet being perceived as frustratingly indecisive). Despite the chaos of his thoughts, he reverts to societal norms of behaviour to challenge the ghost's true nature. Hamlet's chosen medium for factual realisation is often known as 'the play within the play' – the performance requested of 'The Mousetrap', a play designed to reveal 'the [true] conscience of the King'. This introduces the idea of *true* and *false* consciousnesses, implying that Hamlet is not the only one being deceptive. Claudius, similarly, has masked his individual desires for his brother's wife and his power, adopting a performance intended to fool the Danish people.

However, Blake reached a new pinnacle of understanding upon creation of *The Marriage of Heaven and Hell* near the end of the eighteenth century. Blake recognised the importance of embracing both the light and dark elements of the human psyche, taking a revolutionary approach to the construction of identity. In order to provide a true representation of our duality, Blake assigns characteristics of the human identity to corresponding, Jung-like archetypal symbols. He uses these to create a series of pairs containing opposing forces, such as 'Good' and 'Evil'. He believes that these polarities are at work in every individual and their disharmonious union is essential to our existence. Blake believed

---

[10] *Hamlet*, Act I, Scene III, ln21

that both of these elements of the identity should be given equal rights to influence an individual's behaviour and to deny this fact is to only half-exist. He sees the suppression of perceived faults, destructive tendencies and perverse desires as a weakness ('those who restrain desire do so because theirs is weak enough to be restrained'[11]). He places as much emphasis on the importance of negative traits as he does on more universally favourable characteristics. It is interesting to note that the identities of the two opposing princes constructed in *Beowulf* and *Hamlet* slot neatly into the roles Blake assigns to the conflicting forces in play in each individual being. These two texts provide excellent examples of how two strongly defined identities can oppose one another. This is an *essential* element of Blake's construction of feuding archetypes, for 'these two classes… should [always] be enemies… [and attempting] to reconcile them seeks to destroy existence'[12]. Beowulf is a Type 1 Personality: this 'portion of being'[13] is represented in various metaphorical forms. Some of these are rather obscure, such as 'Power', 'The Prolific'[14], 'Love'[15] and 'Heaven'[16]. The more tangible of these are animals. The most notable is the 'Lion', but there is also mention of 'the Tyger, the Horse [and] the Elephant'[17]. The two most significant traits of this archetypal lion must be his

---

[11] W. Blake, *The Marriage of Heaven and Hell* in *The Complete Illuminated Books* (London: Thames & Hudson, 2000), plate 5

[12] *The Marriage of Heaven and Hell,* plates 16-17

[13] *The Marriage of Heaven and Hell,* plate 16

[14] *The Marriage of Heaven and Hell,* plate 16

[15] *The Marriage of Heaven and Hell,* plate 3

[16] *The Marriage of Heaven and Hell,* plate 3

[17] *The Marriage of Heaven and Hell,* plate 8

courage and his societal tendencies. Evidence of these implied characteristics are ample in our modern society: one could have a 'lionheart', for example, or be 'leader of the pack', or pride. Lions are fierce and primitive hunters: they rely on their strength and instinct, using it to dominate their territory. If you transport the scene to Lord Hrothgar's main hall, it is not difficult to imagine a pride of Geats! Beowulf is the Alpha Male in a strong and proud band of warriors that share his brute strength. This identity is defined by action rather than thought. Beowulf *needs* his pack to survive – his glory requires company. The courageous acts he has performed alone are not sufficient without his subsequent reputation: he cannot be recognised fully without it. His identity belongs to – and is created by – the society he represents, and it can be filtered and altered by the public that he serves. His society's interpretation of his deeds controls the identity he is assigned: the *real* Beowulf is the man they praise in their songs and boasts[18], a man of awe-inspiring strength and unwavering courage (who renounces his weapons to engage Grendel in hand-to-hand combat[19]/[20]), the man that 'God provides for'[21].

Insofar as identity is created by the text, the omission of certain undesirable characteristics (such as cowardice or grief) effectively erases them from existence. During his banter with Unferth in the main hall[22], Beowulf effectively re-writes history, adapting the tale

---

[18] *Beowulf* (bilingual edition), lns419-424
[19] *Beowulf* (bilingual edition), lns677-687
[20] *Beowulf* (bilingual edition), lns434-439
[21] *The Marriage of Heaven and Hell*, plate 9

to best reflect his strength, competitiveness and fearlessness. Perceived weakness on his part would dishonour the whole tribe. However, Hamlet – Beowulf's counterpart – denies his Type 1 Personality dominance and disregards the demands of his society. Instead of embracing his social position, Hamlet allows his Type 2 Personality to dominate. This is the individual self. Hamlet is the 'Hell' to Beowulf's corresponding 'Heaven'[23], 'the Devouring' to pair 'the Prolific'[24]; he is 'Submission' and 'Hate'[25]. Blake also controversially declared that this portion of the self is, in essence, 'Evil' – however, this word has vastly different connotations to its biblical twin. Blake defines 'Good' and 'Evil' in a radical way: he suggests that 'Good is the passive that obeys Reason [and] Evil is the action springing from Energy'[26]. Blake symbolises these traits using the '[Cunning][27] Fox[28]'. Hamlet is the 'Shame' to folly Beowulf's 'Pride'[29]. Instead of the clear-cut, justifiable battles Beowulf is offered, Hamlet must instead face a tactical, undefined, psychological battle of wits. Hamlet must find within himself the resources to commit the act of murder and the tangible proof to justify it: 'God provides for the lion, [but] the fox [must] provide for himself'. The deliberate, deceptive performance of a false identity that Hamlet undertakes to achieve this challenge accepted norms of

[22] *Beowulf* (bilingual edition), lns499-606
[23] *The Marriage of Heaven and Hell*, plate 3
[24] *The Marriage of Heaven and Hell*, plate 16
[25] *The Marriage of Heaven and Hell*, plate 3
[26] *The Marriage of Heaven and Hell*, plate 3
[27] *The Marriage of Heaven and Hell*, plate 10
[28] *The Marriage of Heaven and Hell*, plate 8
[29] *The Marriage of Heaven and Hell*, plate 7

behaviour. Where vengeance enacted by Beowulf in response to the deaths caused by his foes is celebrated and governed publicly by the laws of the blood feud[30], Hamlet's is a shameful secret. The princes are united in action but divided by thought.

To compile the two opposing identities as Blake suggested would free their minds: one would be able to see 'genius... [in] torture and insanity'[31]; see with a wise man's eyes what a fool's cannot[32]. Perhaps this would allow Hamlet to gather the courage to act before his mother was poisoned[33], or save Beowulf from inevitable death in the pursuit of glory[34]. To me, Blake's text demonstrates a striking insight into the human consciousness and approaches the construction of identity in a way that is unrivalled. It attempts to justify the true horrors of the world: infant death, violence, greed, war. Blake's abandonment of God and His constraints has allowed him passage through a world onto which both Heaven *and* Hell have been superimposed. Its detached honesty provides freedom to the individual being.

---

[30] S. Heaney, 'Introduction' in *Beowulf* (bilingual edition), (London: Faber and Faber, 2007) , pp. xiv-xv
[31] *The Marriage of Heaven and Hell*, plate 6
[32] *The Marriage of Heaven and Hell*, plate 7
[33] *Hamlet*, Act V, Scene II, lns263-264
[34] *Beowulf* (bilingual edition), lns3383-1396

The Sonnet and Its Blurred Boundaries
(An Analysis of Paterson's *101 Sonnets)*

When Paterson declared that 'the sonnet is... in the eye of the beholder'[35], he meant that the recognition of a sonnet's authenticity – or the denial of its status as a *real* sonnet – is based on the subjective opinions of learned individuals, as the 'definitive boundaries... [of] the form... [have] diversified to the point that [they] effectively cease to exist'[36]. There are five agreed characteristics which sonnets typically demonstrate which help to determine whether a poem is *really* a sonnet or simply a 'quatorzain'[37]. In order to be considered a sonnet, the text should have fourteen lines. It should be written in iambic pentameter, adhere to a recognisable rhyme scheme and demonstrate a change of direction in the narrative, marked by the volta. Finally, it should address the subject of the romantic, celestial and sublime. Increasingly, though, these governing rules have become guidelines: poets have experimented with them beyond the point of recognition, causing disagreements amongst scholars as to what a sonnet *is*. Attempts to regulate the form and filter out fraudulent poems are ludicrous, creating restrictions 'so fascistic that they would cheerfully exclude

---

[35] Don Paterson, 'Introduction', in *101 Sonnets*, ed. by Don Paterson (London: Faber and Faber, 1999), p. xi
[36] Paterson, 'Introduction', p. xi
[37] J. A. Cuddon, 'Quatorzain', in *The Penguin Dictionary of Literary Terms & Literary Theory* (fourth edition), rev. by C. E. Preston (London: Penguin Books, 1999), p.719

all the work of Shakespeare or Wordsworth'[38]. So, it is important to note that some of these rules can be bent or broken. Paterson writes that 'every really good sonnet seems to ignore at least one of the so-called rules'[39]. After all, 'form alone [cannot] create art'[40], and the structure is intended to provide the writer with 'a theatre rather than a prison'[41].

Poets brave enough to experiment with the form often strengthen the art. Spenser's deviation from pre-defined norms, for example, resulted in the creation of a new rhyme scheme (ababbcbccdcdee, demonstrated in *Faerie Queen*[42]).The sonnet has transformed and evolved spectacularly through its fairly brief history of just over 750 years. During its development it has produced two main, recognisable forms: Italian and English. The sonnet originally came from Italian roots that stretch back to the early thirteenth century. The poet Lentino is attributed with its earliest known usage, but the Italian form is often referred to as 'Petrarchan', named after the poet that perfected the art in his cycle, *Canzoniere*[43]. At this point, sonnets were mainly concerned with one subject: love. Poets

[38] Paterson, 'Introduction', p. xii
[39] Paterson, 'Introduction', p. xii
[40] Natalie Goldberg, *Writing Down the Bones: Freeing the Writer Within*, (London: Shambhala, 2005), p.134
[41] M. Ferguson, 'Versification', in *The Norton Anthology of Poetry* (fifth edition), ed. by M. Ferguson, M. Salter & J. Stallworthy (London: W. W. Norton & Company, 2005), p.2042
[42] Edmund Spenser, 'The First Booke' of *The Faerie Queen*, in *The Norton Anthology of Poetry* (fifth edition), ed. by M. Ferguson, M. Salter & J. Stallworthy (London: W. W. Norton & Company, 2005), pp.165-192
[43] Petrarch (translated by A. S. Kline), *Canzoniere* (Poetry In Translation, 2002) <http://tkline.p.cc.net/PITBR/ Italian/Petrarchhome.htm>

obsessed over the pursuit of its beauty, the recording of its blossom and the mourning of its demise. However, Paterson observes that 'this was often used as a pretext to write about a far wider variety of subjects – time, death, eternity and the imagination'[44]. Its rhyme scheme and structure are relatively simple. The poem is divided into two parts: the first eight lines 'comprise the octave... and rhyme abbaabba; the following six lines, or sestet, usually rhyme cdecde... [but] rhyme variations are admissible'[45], such as cdcdcd (used by d'Arezzo amongst others). The octave presents a 'theme or problem... [and] the sestet resolves [this statement]'[46] or observation with 'a counter-statement... [or] amplifying conclusion'[47]. This chosen division (8:6) is demonstrated in all the arts[48], and is known as 'the golden ratio'. Wordsworth paid tribute to the rhyme scheme set out by the Italians in his poem, 'The World Is Too Much With Us'[49] and demonstrates this expansion of topic. In abandoning romantic positivity and instead choosing to use the form to express his frustrations, he addresses not unrequited love but his soulless, Christian existence. He expresses a desire to return to a purer, simpler state of being: something he mirrors by reverting to the sonnet's original, Italian form. He honours its tendency to obey the

---

[44] Paterson, 'Introduction', p. xiv
[45] Cuddon, 'Petrarchan Sonnet', pp.661-662
[46] Cuddon, 'Petrarchan Sonnet', pp.661-662
[47] Ferguson, 'Versification', p.2042
[48] Paterson, 'Introduction', p. xviii
[49] W. Wordsworth, 'The World Is Too Much With Us', in *Romanticism: An Anthology* (third edition), ed. by Duncan Wu (Oxford: Blackwell Publishing, 2006), p.534

golden ratio, beginning with a statement in the opening octave and closing with an amplifying conclusion in the final sestet. Yet, he expresses hesitancy by delaying the volta slightly (halfway through ln9, at 'Great God!'[50], marked distinctly with a hyphen) and mimics 'wrestling with the meter'[51] to show his frustration by reversing the opening iambs of lns2-3, starting with a stressed syllable and disrupting the sonnet's rhythm slightly.

The Italian sonnet was just the beginning of our relationship with this form. Wyatt introduced the English to the sonnet in the sixteenth century, resulting in the innovation of the English form. It is alternately known as the 'Shakespearian' form, for obvious reasons. This type of sonnet is typically written in 'iambic pentameters… consisting of three quatrains and a concluding couplet [with]… a rhyme scheme… [of] ababcdcdefefgg'[52]. Shakespeare's importance as a sonneteer cannot be ignored and as such it is hard to analyse his work by focusing on just one sonnet. I have chosen 'Sonnet 15'[53] due to its 'dissembled approach'[54] to subject matter. Shakespeare uses the topic of love as a pretext to examine human frailty in the face of time. His loyal adherence to iambic pentameter gives this poem a song-like quality which is uplifting even in the face of its

---

[50] Wordsworth, 'The World Is Too Much With Us', ln9

[51] Don Paterson, 'Notes', in *101 Sonnets,* ed. by Don Paterson (London: Faber and Faber, 1999), p.105

[52] Cuddon, 'Shakespearian Sonnet', pp.813-814

[53] William Shakespeare, 'Sonnet 15', in *William Shakespeare: The Complete Works* (second edition), ed. by Stanley Wells and Gary Taylor (Oxford: Oxford University Press, 2005), p.780

[54] Paterson, 'Introduction', p. xiv

melancholic message. He attempts to capture his lover's brief moment of 'perfection'[55], in which she is 'rich in youth'[56], before she decays and is wasted by time[57]. Shakespeare's work 'liberated poets thereafter to speak…directly'[58]. Milton 'widened its scope, addressing political subjects and writing deeply personal sonnets of elegy and confession'[59]. His poem, 'When I Consider How My Life Is Spent'[60], is a bitter, autobiographical reflection on the author's loss of sight and his inner questioning of the divine justice which has meant half his life has been 'spent… in [a] dark world'[61]. He mirrors Patience's haste to 'prevent [his] murmur [of discontent]'[62] with his fate using 'an accelerated turn… in the last line of the octave'[63] (at 'but Patience…'[64]), providing a wonderful example of how content can dictate form.

Not all sonnets can be attributed easily to a given category. Hybrid and overlapping variations, such as the 'Anglo-Italian' sonnet, were bound to emerge. Drayton's 'Since There's No Help, Come Let Us Kiss and Part'[65] is a fine example of how a sonnet's form can be

---

[55] Shakespeare, 'Sonnet 15', ln2
[56] Shakespeare, 'Sonnet 15', ln10
[57] Shakespeare, 'Sonnet 15, ln11
[58] Paterson, 'Introduction', p. xiv
[59] Paterson, 'Introduction', p. xiv
[60] John Milton, 'When I Consider How My Life Is Spent', in *The Norton Anthology of Poetry* (fifth edition), ed. by M. Ferguson, M. Salter & J. Stallworthy (London: W. W. Norton & Company, 2005), p.418
[61] Milton, 'When I Consider How My Life Is Spent', lns1-2
[62] Milton, 'When I Consider How My Life Is Spent', lns8-9
[63] Ferguson, 'Versification', p.2042
[64] Milton, 'When I Consider How My Life Is Spent', ln8
[65] Michael Drayton, 'Since There's No Help, Come Let Us Kiss and Part', in *101*

open to interpretation and debate. Drayton's poem uses a traditional English rhyme scheme, follows the conventional form of three quatrains accompanied by a closing couplet and is written (with the exception of the couplet) in iambic pentameter. According to Abrams, it is unmistakably written in Shakespearian style. He eloquently describes how 'the lover brusquely declares in the first two quatrains that he is glad the affair is cleanly broken off, pauses in the third quatrain as though at the threshold, and in the last two lines suddenly drops his swagger to make one last plea'[66]. However, Paterson provides a different interpretation of its layout and structure, acknowledging the presence of an octave and sestet formation more commonly found in Italian variations. Paterson believes the lover puts on 'a brave face of the octave... [before] the poet's resolve wavers and collapses entirely in the sestet'[67]. The pause at the start of the third quatrain is interpreted instead as the poem's volta, turning at 'now at the last gap of Love's latest breath'[68]. Postmodernist poets have muddied the waters further, re-defining the sonnet's purpose and adapting the form beyond recognition. It can no longer be defined by the rigid set of regulations outlined earlier. Thomas' contribution to Paterson's collection, 'Their Faces Shone Under Some Radiance'[69], provides an excellent example of

---

Sonnets, ed. by Don Paterson (London: Faber and Faber, 1999), p.53

[66] M. H. Abrams, 'Versification', in *The Norton Anthology of Poetry* (fifth edition), ed. by M. Ferguson, M. Salter & J. Stallworthy (London: W. W. Norton & Company, 2005), p.2044

[67] Paterson, 'Notes', p.112

[68] Drayton, 'Since There's No Help, Come Let Us Kiss and Part', ln9

[69] Dylan Thomas, 'Their Faces Shone Under Some Radiance', in *101 Sonnets*, ed.

how a sonnet's status could be debated. This poem breaks more agreed rules than it follows and one could easily argue that it is not a sonnet at all. It is scattered with occasional half-rhymes, the most notable pairing being 'replying'[70] and 'dying'[71]. Its structure is chaotic (but not necessarily disorganised) and completely defies Paterson's 'little squared circle'[72] poem philosophy. Its sentence length and syllabic meter varies considerably, the volta is late (occurring at ln10, starting at 'before the moon shifted'[73]) and its closing couplet does not rhyme, although it *does* signify a melancholic end to the event as 'the light, which temporarily held death at bay, [withdraws]'[74]. Even the topic chosen rejects convention. Thomas' cynical account certainly rips off the readers' rose-tinted glasses, showing them meaningless, 'empty kisses'[75] and a girl in a 'cheap frock'[76] instead of a declaration of love. However, he seems touched by the momentary enchantment that enriches the surroundings momentarily before 'the suicides parade again'[77], albeit an artificial magic.

Each of these texts help to illustrate the point that Paterson was trying to make with this enlightening collection of poetry: the sonnet

---

by Don Paterson (London: Faber and Faber, 1999), p.55
[70] Thomas, 'Their Faces Shone Under Some Radiance', ln12
[71] Thomas, 'Their Faces Shone Under Some Radiance', ln14
[72] Paterson, 'Introduction', p. xvi
[73] Thomas, 'Their Faces Shone Under Some Radiance', ln10
[74] Paterson, 'Notes', p.112
[75] Thomas, 'Their Faces Shone Under Some Radiance', ln3
[76] Thomas, 'Their Faces Shone Under Some Radiance', ln11
[77] Thomas, 'Their Faces Shone Under Some Radiance', ln14

is not an 'arbitrary construct that poets pit themselves against… it's a box for their dreams… [representing] one of the most characteristic shapes human thought can take'[78]. With this in mind, the clinical regulation of this art and the attempts to exclude poets' works because they deviate from the norm is counter-productive and shows naivety of the sonnet's purpose as a tool for aesthetic expression. The precedents set by great poets must not be ignored, but attempting to cage ideas within an inflexible structure is foolish: poetry is an art, after all, not a science.

---

[78] Paterson, 'Introduction', p. xxvii

The Revelation or Concealment of Reality
(Plato Versus Aristotle)

In order to examine the representation of reality in literary texts, the very nature of reality must be questioned. It is impossible to discuss to what degree the 'real' can be revealed to, or concealed from, its audience without first agreeing upon the standard of 'real'. The modern-day consensus would define reality as the material world surrounding us – that is, the world of appearances that we all experience through our senses. This agreement carries the implication that literary texts, like other art forms, may recreate elements taken from physical reality through the act of 'mimesis'[79], but their representations in the text will always differ somewhat from the 'real' because it is impossible to fully express the original in its entirety.

This may seem an obvious statement, but it is significant to draw attention to the fact that it would be impossible for a writer to recreate a door, for example, in its most complete form. Modern structuralists would preach that although the use of the agreed symbol 'D-O-O-R' may adequately ensure that the audience is familiar with the subject matter, but no matter how detailed the description of the door's sturdiness or accurate the representation of

---

[79] 'Mimesis', in *The Penguin Dictionary of Literary Terms and Literary Theory*, ed. by J.A. Cuddon (London: Penguin, 1998), p.512

its wood, the audience would never be able to shelter behind that door because it is constructed of nothing more than words. The writer's door is not a 'real' door: it is a second-hand perception, expressed by an imperfect system of signifiers. This has led some of the greatest minds ever recorded to distrust the act of artistic representation because it cannot adequately reveal what is 'real'. The concept of reality was even more complex at the birth of recorded intellectual thought, owing to the philosophical notion that the physical world is not the true reality.

Plato, who is often credited as the forefather of the tradition of literary criticism and theory although evidence exists that many of the ideas he explores were established in his philosophical community, expressed this view. He subsequently placed 'representation and truth... a considerable distance apart'[80] and stated that poetry and art sought to conceal the truth on more than one level. He thought that objects in the material world were 'mutable'[81] representations of true Objects, existing in a 'realm of unchanging being'[82] completely independent of our own. These are known as 'Forms' or 'Ideas' and express the objects in their purest, most 'real' state. This led him to see artists and poets as 'imitators of imitations'[83], removed three times from the essential nature of

---

[80] Plato, 'Poetry and Unreality', in *Republic*, trans. by R. Waterfield (Oxford: Oxford World Classics, 1993), p.348

[81] Leitch, Vincent, 'Plato' in *The Norton Anthology of Theory and Criticism* (first edition), ed. by V. Leitch, W. Cain, L. Finke & B. Johnson (London: WW Norton & Co, 2001), p.33

[82] Leitch, 'Plato', p.34

[83] Selden, Raman, 'Imaginative Representation', in *The Theory of Criticism, from*

what is 'real'. He saw the act of mimetic representation of nature as a lifeless deviation that led 'away from the truth'[84] and gave the audience a 'distorted image of the nature of the gods'[85]. Plato subsequently chose to deliver the majority of his texts in the form of philosophical debate, believing that 'anamnesis'[86], the 'genuine, living wisdom'[87] of philosophy, allowed for a deeper interaction with the 'essential Form of Goodness'[88] governing the realm of true Ideas. This certainly enables him to express a myriad of views, and his use of multiple characters brought on by a seeming reluctance to speak in his own voice (although he heavily favours his primary 'mouthpiece'[89] Socrates) means that he can create a duality of opinion. Plato is then free to challenge his own ideas, and argue for both sides of the debate. This is a more accurate demonstration of how humans interact with each other and our world, which Plato believed brought philosophers a step closer to the truth. In fact, Plato demoted the representations of artists and poets should be demoted to less than that of a craftsman, as their knowledge of their subject matter is inferior to 'that of charioteers, fishermen and philosophers'[90], as a mere 'representer [knows] nothing of the value about the things

---

Plato to the Present: A Reader, ed. by R. Selden (Harlow: Pearson Education, 1988), p.9

[84] Leitch, 'Plato', p.33

[85] Plato, *Republic*, in *The Norton Anthology of Theory and Criticism* (first edition), ed. by V. Leitch, W. Cain, L. Finke & B. Johnson (London: WW Norton & Co, 2001), p.50

[86] 'Anamnesis', in *The Penguin Dictionary of Literary Terms and Literary Theory*, ed. by J.A. Cuddon (London: Penguin, 1998), p.36

[87] Leitch, 'Plato', p.36

[88] Selden, *The Theory of Criticism, from Plato to the Present: A Reader*, p.9

[89] Leitch, 'Plato', p.34

[90] Leitch, 'Plato', p.35

he represents'[91] when compared to the true 'Maker' (God), or even the human manufacturer. To demonstrate, Plato uses the analogy of the three beds. He believed that the physical act of making a bed was purer, or more 'real', than an artist's depiction of the same bed. However, both beds would pale in comparison to God's original bed. Plato advised that the only way for the poet to escape his 'lying' nature and experience the same genuine, divine inspiration as the philosopher and gain access to the only 'real' Ideas, he must enter a state of 'divine madness'[92] and vacate his physical mind, allowing something greater to form within it. In this state, he concedes that the poet may be able to provide an insight (albeit limited) into the true nature of the world surrounding us. Otherwise, though, the poet and artist are placed firmly at the lowest level of cognition on his Line. He even suggested that poets should be banished from his idealised republic, an idea met with some hostility. To comment on the use, suitability and morality of poetry was to comment on Greek culture and society as a whole. It frequently used the 'mnemonic devices'[93] of poetry and music to pass on their knowledge, meaning poets were considered to be the 'educators of Greece'[94]. Plato thought that this respected and powerful position should belong to the philosophers

---

[91] Plato, 'Book X', in *The Norton Anthology of Theory and Criticism* (first edition), ed. by V. Leitch, W. Cain, L. Finke & B. Johnson (London: WW Norton & Co, 2001), p.70
[92] Plato, *Ion*, in *The Norton Anthology of Theory and Criticism* (first edition), ed. by V. Leitch, W. Cain, L. Finke & B. Johnson (London: WW Norton & Co, 2001), p.41
[93] Leitch, 'Plato', pp.35-36
[94] Waterfield, Robin, 'Introduction', in *Republic*, ed. & trans. by R. Waterfield (Oxford: Oxford World Classics, 1993), p. xxx

instead, perhaps the first evidence of the rift that was to form between philosophy and poetry.

His determination to ensure that poetry and art adhered to a rigid moral standard caused him to encourage the censorship of any poetry considered 'sacrilegious, sentimental, unlawful or irrational'[95]. In 'Book III' of *Republic*, he recommends that the portrayal of mourning, grief and death should be edited. Even names that may cause fear (such as 'Cocytus' or 'Styx') should likewise be removed. This restriction would diminish the range and creative powers of the poet by limiting the representation of probably the most frightening, mysterious and emotive topics any human being could address – our own mortality. Plato felt poets were unsuitable to tackle such an intangible, abstract and universal subject, and one so closely connected to God. It is unsurprising, then, to note that succeeding Platonists deflect attention away from his rejection of the poets' ability to adequately represent the 'real'. Plotinus, the founder of the neo-Platonic school of philosophy, achieved this by elevating art to the top of the cognitive ladder, describing it as a direct interaction with the essential Form of 'Intellectual Beauty'[96]. By denying that art is 'merely the pale imitation of a more perfect nature'[97], Selden notes how this reversal allows art to become an expression of 'the

---

[95] Leitch, 'Plato', p.36
[96] Plotinus, 'Eighth Tractate: On the Intellectual Beauty', in *The Norton Anthology of Theory and Criticism* (first edition), ed. by V. Leitch, W. Cain, L. Finke & B. Johnson (London: WW Norton & Co, 2001), p.174
[97] Leitch, 'Plotinus', in *The Norton Anthology of Theory and Criticism* (first edition), ed. by V. Leitch, W. Cain, L. Finke & B. Johnson (London: WW Norton & Co, 2001), p.171

essential Form of the Good and the Beautiful'[98], permitting the artist to 'access the world of intelligible Forms [instead of] languishing in the world of appearances'[99]. This implies a much closer relationship with the truth (and its governor) than the one Plato describes.

The most influential theory to challenge Plato's view of representation originated from Aristotle. *Poetics* also addresses the act of mimesis, but the term does not carry the same negative connotations as it does in Plato's work. *Poetics* responds to Plato's criticisms of poetry by offering a 'stable theory of poetry's true nature'[100] and purpose. Although the two philosophers are loosely united by the idea that mimesis should have some form of correspondence with reality, Aristotle differs on a vital issue: that of *possibility*. The poet is not bound to just represent things as they are now, or once were. He is able to use mimesis to portray that which '*may* happen'[101] or things that 'ought to be'[102]. Halliwell points out how Aristotle's acknowledgement that 'art offers images of *possible* reality… involves a crucial relaxation'[103] of Platonic demands for absolute truth. Aristotle does not hold poets accountable to the same 'fixed criterion of truth [and] reality' as philosophers and historians,

---

[98] Selden, Raman, *The Theory of Criticism, from Plato to the Present: A Reader*, ed. by R. Selden (Harlow, Pearson Education, 1988), p.9
[99] Selden, *The Theory of Criticism, from Plato the Present: A Reader*, p.9
[100] Halliwell, Stephen, 'Aristotle's *Poetics*', in *The Cambridge History of Literary Criticism Volume I: Classical Criticism*, ed. by G.A. Kennedy (Cambridge: Cambridge University Press, 1997), p.152
[101] Aristotle, *Poetics*, trans. by S.H. Butcher (New York: Dover Publications, 1997), p.17
[102] Aristotle, *Poetics*, p.17
[103] Halliwell, 'Aristotle's *Poetics*', p.152

despite the fact that all three groups concern themselves with human experiences within the physical world. Practitioners of philosophy and history must strive to report only the 'direct truths' of reality, whether in the more specific sense of historical details or the generalised, universal truths that philosophers deliver. Artists, however, make their *own* world by undergoing a complex mediation of reality in order to represent elements of the 'real' within a recognised aesthetic structure. In Aristotle's view, the process of poetic imitation contained three aspects: means', object' and 'manner'[104]. The *means* is the chosen medium, or what structuralist critics like Jakobson would call the 'contact'[105] method – that is, the framework that the artist agrees to create within. The *object* is that which the artist chooses to represent, after 'rigorous selection'[106]. Finally, the *manner* is the fictional mode of presentation or genre, and dictates the form and style the poet uses. The resulting design is 'a product of art, not a statement or description of existing reality'[107], although it is required to correspond to life within its structural order. This is not to say, though, that poets are not dealing with what is 'real'. On the contrary, Aristotle believed that poetry has a unique ability to reveal a form of truth outside of history's collective reach. Historians are limited to reveal only what *has* happened, whereas the poet is free to explore what *could* happen. Selden notes how

---

[104] Selden, *The Theory of Criticism, from Plato to the Present: A Reader,* p.40
[105] Jakobson, Roman, 'Linguistics and Poetics', in *Modern Criticism and Theory: A Reader*, ed. by D. Lodge (London: Longman, 1988), p.35
[106] Selden, *The Theory of Criticism, from Plato to the Present: A Reader,* p.40
[107] Halliwell, 'Aristotle's *Poetics*', p.153

Aristotle saw the poet's role as one which could transform the possible into the probable by observing the 'unities and rules of probability of their craft'[108]. In doing so, the poet can actually surpass the 'real' by creating something 'possessing a general truthfulness... which fits convincingly into a chain of actions and contributes to a unified, poetic whole'[109]. This is achieved through the correct use of 'Character, Plot, Diction, Song and Thought'[110]. This requires the poet to create order out of the chaos of reality, no longer simply imitating objects or situations occurring in the physical world, but revealing a 'logical coherence underlying events in human life'[111]. This is achieved by successfully constructing a plot consisting of a sequence of actions 'evolving with convincingness and inevitability'[112]. Aristotle thought that great poetry was able to assign 'a beginning, a middle and an end'[113] to history for comedic or tragic effect, eliminating unnecessary elements of the story to retain clarity, and portraying the great men of history as better (or worse) than they were. This gave their story a magnitude that historians, limited to the actual facts, were unable to compete with. Aristotle's concept of mimesis is unavoidably drawn toward the notion of the 'dramatic' and away from the responsibility of bridging the gap between reality and imitation; between the 'real' and the representation.

---

[108] Selden, *The Theory of Criticism, from Plato to the Present: A Reader*, p.78
[109] Selden, *The Theory of Criticism, from Plato to the Present: A Reader*, p.41
[110] Aristotle, *Poetics*, p.11
[111] Selden, *The Theory of Criticism, from Plato to the Present: A Reader*, p.41
[112] Selden, *The Theory of Criticism, from Plato to the Present: A Reader*, p.41
[113] Aristotle, *Poetics*, p.14

The significant difference between the approach of Aristotle and that of Plato resides in which *reality* they choose to draw their conclusions from. Aristotle observes particular objects in the physical world and uses them to draw general conclusions about the state of all things. Plato, however, draws very specific conclusions, but to do so he draws upon his 'general metaphysical concept of being'[114]. Leitch observes that Aristotle works through a process of 'induction'[115], whereas Plato favours 'deduction'[116]. Aristotle provides an advancement of Plato's view that stems from the hope that mimetic representation can surpass the physical world that is bound by the laws of time, history and factual accuracy. Both philosophers agree that mimesis can conceal – that is beyond question – but Aristotle offers it the opportunity to transcend its lowly position and engage in the act of revelation.

---

[114] Leitch, 'Aristotle', in *The Norton Anthology of Theory and Criticism* (first edition), ed. by V. Leitch, W. Cain, L. Finke & B. Johnson (London: WW Norton & Co, 2001), p.87
[115] Leitch, 'Aristotle', p.87
[116] Leitch, 'Aristotle', p.87

Contestation of Britain's Status as a Multi-Racial Nation
(Gilroy's Challenge of High Society)

When Gilroy stated that 'Britain may be a multiracial society but…
may never [become] a multiracial nation'[117], he made a crucial and
revealing distinction between two very different types of
community. In order for a community to be considered a 'society',
the members within it must live in a state of relative order. The
people are required to share little beyond a system of agreed
'customs, laws and [governing] organisations'[118] to qualify for this
status. It is a passive involvement, achieved by simply agreeing to
adhere to the laws of the land. In order for a large community to
evolve into a 'nation' though, a critical progression must take place:
the members must integrate their collective 'culture, language [and]
history'[119], making it inclusive for *all* parties. Despite recent
advances, this unification is still painfully lacking in modern Britain.
Instead of fully embracing its promise of a United Kingdom, Britain
suffers an enduring and uneven distribution of power that has
ensured our historical, cultural and communicative focus remains
firmly in the control of a predominantly white, 'high society'. This
'high society' has shown reluctance to fully acknowledge the
immense pressure-cooker of culture gradually amassing itself in

---

[117] Paul Gilroy – quote taken from assigned essay question (source not cited)
[118] 'Society', in *The Compact Oxford English Dictionary for Students* (third
edition), ed. by C. Soanes (Oxford: Oxford University Press, 2006), p.984
[119] 'Nation', in *The Compact Oxford English Dictionary for Students* (third
edition), ed. by C. Soanes (Oxford: Oxford University Press, 2006), p.675

Britain after the series of black diasporic movements from Africa, Southern Asia and the Caribbean initiated in the early post-war period. They have become a restricted 'low society', and those with power, wealth and influence are not keen to relinquish the elevated status they currently enjoy over this collective group. Disruptions to their established grand narrative are unwelcome because, according to Hall, they directly challenge the 'decisive mental repression… [and selective] historical amnesia… [among] the British people'[120].

Instead, in what Procter views as a direct avoidance of 'the messy, unsettled politics'[121] of the present day, the year 1948 – specifically, the arrival of the *SS Windrush* – is often represented as the singular defining moment of completed sequence of events no longer requiring consideration. An organic community is collectively reduced to a single moment in time: 'the year in which a single boat docked at Tilbury'[122], disregarding any post-war black British presence before that moment. The pre-war black British presence is more thoroughly historicised but extremely detached, accentuating the separation of black communities from British society. Brennan's collective summary acknowledges 'the Moorish soldiers of Hadrian's army, the African entertainers of the Tudor court… [and] the writers of the great emancipation autobiographies'[123], but all

[120] Stuart Hall, 'Racism and Reaction', in *Five Views of Multi-Cultural Britain* (London: Commission for Racial Equality, 1978), p.25
[121] James Procter, 'General Introduction: 1948-1998 – Periodising Postwar Black Britain', in *Writing Black Britain: 1948-1998*, ed. by J. Procter (Manchester: Manchester University Press, 2000), p.2
[122] Procter, 'General Introduction', p.3
[123] Timothy Brennan, 'Writing from Black Britain', *Literary Review*, 34 (autumn

emphasis is placed of what makes them *different* from the British, not a part of their history or culture. The *Windrush* has become a convenient symbol of the black presence, ritually reported in the national media as welcomed[124]. In truth, the men and women of different race, origin and class aboard were greeted by a country already reluctant to incorporate them. Regardless of the lack of historical recognition of its cultural importance though, their arrival 'constitutes a distinct phase of black British history... [producing] a community whose difference from... earlier black Britons cannot be underestimated'[125]. These initial settlements in the 1940s and 1950s led to the emergence of a distinct and specifically 'black' British cultural identity, already possessing the elements required to establish a multiracial nation. The immigrants brought with them a rich, diverse array of collective languages, histories and cultures which they willingly shared with one another. The failure to properly integrate them into the 'white' nation is due to the 'high society' exercising their 'capacity to evacuate any historical dimension to black life'[126], a 'fundamental achievement of racist ideologies in [Britain]'[127]. As a result, this 'early phase of cultural production'[128] in the immediate post-war period has been poorly

1990), p.7
[124] Peter Fryer, *Staying Power: The History of Black People in Britain* (London: Pluto Press, 1984), p.372
[125] Procter, 'General Introduction', p.4
[126] Paul Gilroy, *There Ain't No Black in the Union Jack – The Cultural Politics of Race and Nation* (London: Routledge, 1987), p.11
[127] Gilroy, *There Ain't No Black in the Union Jack*, p.11
[128] James Procter, 'Part One: 1948 to late 1960s', in *Writing Black Britain: 1948-1998*, ed. by J. Procter (Manchester: Manchester University Press, 2000), p.13

documented – and the literature produced by it largely ignored – until a recent renewal in academic interest was prompted by the approach of the *Windrush*'s fiftieth anniversary. Black literature from this period is dominated by the West Indian male writers who settled in London and the surrounding areas in the 1950s. Some were drawn to the literary capital by the opportunity of mass publication and circulation of their work, on a previously 'unimaginable'[129] scale. Others, like Selvon, came seeking employment in the British manufacturing and service industries, responding to the country's promotion of black immigration in a bid to counter non-skilled labour shortages. It is during this *'laissez-faire'* phase of black British history immediately after the introduction of the Nationality Act (1948) that Selvon produced the only 'black' text of the period to be successfully circulated until the anniversary celebrations[130] – *The Lonely Londoners.* In this text, he explores the obstacles and issues facing the black community in what is often mistakenly portrayed as a benign, cooperative initial phase. At the time of writing this text, the black community were already being policed and monitored, albeit unofficially. They also quickly became the focus of the media, whose over-anxious and increasingly paranoid surveillance fanned the flames of national distrust. Selvon was well aware of this growing resentment, fuelled by the media's negative portrayal of the increasing black population. His protagonist, Moses, is wary of the 'newspapers and radio [that] rule this country…

---

[129] Procter, 'Part One: 1948 to late 1960s', p.13
[130] Procter, 'General Introduction', p.9

[saying] the West Indians think… the streets of London are paved with gold'[131]. However, not all of the new arrivals are as perceptive. Whilst waiting for Galahad at Waterloo, Moses encounters Tolroy greeting his disembarking family. When an *Echo* reporter tries to interview Tanty, she ironically labels Tolroy's discouragement as 'prejudice'[132] and poses for a family photograph, oblivious to the malice until their image is used to warn of the threat of Jamaican families infiltrating Britain[133], settling rather than filling temporary labour shortages. She perceives the reporter as part of some imagined welcome committee, but the interaction holds a sinister foreboding of the troubles to come.

Despite the natives' unfriendliness, evidence suggests that the pioneering black settlers tried to assimilate themselves and embrace all aspects of the British culture. In 'Reconstruction Work', Hall describes the black people disembarking from trains in tailored suits, trying to imitate British codes of dress and conduct[134]. These early attempts at assimilation are recorded by Selvon, too, in examples of black men dressing 'like Englishmen, [complete] with hat… umbrella [and] *The Times*'[135].

---

[131] Sam Selvon, *The Lonely Londoners* (London: Penguin Books, 2006), p.2
[132] Selvon, *The Lonely Londoners*, p.10
[133] Selvon, *The Lonely Londoners*, p.10
[134] Stuart Hall, 'Reconstruction Work: Images of Postwar Black Settlement', in *Writing Black Britain: 1948-1998* ed. by J. Procter (Manchester: Manchester University Press, 2000), pp.82-94
[135] Selvon, *The Lonely Londoners*, p.137

These early communities still held a sense of cultural idolisation of the United Kingdom, taking great pleasure in using iconic sites as meeting places and reference points, particularly 'symbolic venues'[136] of departure and arrival. Daniel gets a 'big kick… [from escorting white women] to Covent Garden {or] Festival Hall'[137]. Bartholomew is 'always talking about this party or that meeting… in the West End or in Park Lane'[138]. Galahad, too, falls victim to the 'big romance'[139] of these place names, deliberately scheduling dates 'by Charing Cross'[140], or 'the big clock… in Piccadilly Tube Station'[141], and even visiting Waterloo Bridge[142] because of the iconic film. The black communities of early post-war Britain soon learned, though, that their settlement here would not be without certain conditions. The imposing nature of the 'colour bar' demonstrate flaws present in the supposed ''equality' shown between black and white citizens'[143]. The primary sources of national anxiety at this point in history, according to Gilroy[144] and Hall[145], were misgivings about so-called ''miscegenation'' (itself a racist term) and the desire to restrict the availability of black accommodation. As a result, the black

---

[136] Procter, 'General Introduction', p.15
[137] Selvon, *The Lonely Londoners*, p.43
[138] Selvon, *The Lonely Londoners*, p.46
[139] Selvon, *The Lonely Londoners*, p.71
[140] Selvon, *The Lonely Londoners*, p.71
[141] Selvon, *The Lonely Londoners*, p.72
[142] Selvon, *The Lonely Londoners*, p.72
[143] Learie Constantine, 'Colour Bar', in *Writing Black Britain: 1948-1998,* ed. by J. Procter (Manchester: Manchester University Press, 2000), p.68
[144] Paul Gilroy, 'Blacks and Crime in Postwar Britain', in *Writing Black Britain: 1948-1998,* ed. by J. Procter (Manchester: Manchester University Press, 2000), pp.71-77
[145] Hall, 'Reconstruction Work: Images of Postwar Black Settlement', pp.82-94

community found itself 'virtually obliged'[146] to live in poor, distinctly 'black' areas, which were often made up of slums, bedsits and overcrowded houses, in a state of forced inferiority. Members of the 'high society' were reluctant to share their restaurants, jobs and neighbourhoods with black people[147], regardless of class or background. Inter-racial relationships rarely progressed beyond short sexual encounters (unsurprising, considering the associated scandal and exclusion). The increasing restrictions and prejudice prevented the formation of a successful, multiracial nation at its most basic levels.

The Lonely Londoners is rich with examples of the 'colour bar' in practice. Moses recounts how although exclusion is not explicitly stated, when entering a hotel or restaurant 'they will politely tell you to haul... [and] give you the cold treatment'[148]. He tells Galahad of a Polish restaurant, 'the Rendezvous Restaurant [in Ipswich]'[149], where 'foreigners' still refuse to serve black British subjects, and of his friend's encounter with a notice pleading to 'Keep the Water White'[150]. Selvon also provides the reader with an insight into the poor, cramped living conditions of black, working-class 1950s London. His description of Tolroy's family's accommodation on Harrow Road reveals a community nearing poverty[151]. However

---

[146] Constantine, 'Colour Bar', p.65
[147] Constantine, 'Colour Bar', p.67
[148] Selvon, *The Lonely Londoners*, p.21
[149] Selvon, *The Lonely Londoners*, p.21
[150] Selvon, *The Lonely Londoners*, p.77
[151] Selvon, *The Lonely Londoners*, pp.59-60

poor the housing was, it quickly became the place in which black communities felt most welcome. The basements and bedsits of the 'black' slums, although 'sites of exclusion or incarceration, [also became] …important symbolic venues at which the local black community [could freely] congregate'[152]. Black British literature reflected this adaptation of cultural habit, meaning 'basements, bedsits, guest houses, and terraces become repetitious referents within these writings'[153]. Moses observes how his living quarters are a gathering place of cultural safety comparable to a church[154]. Selvon's text is indicative of the growing wariness of the black community upon realisation of the failure of the new, 'united' nation. Prompted by the issue of housing, perhaps more than any other, black Britons began to 'organise and politicise themselves'[155]. The early actions taken by the 'high society' to restrict their perceived inferiors clearly pre-empt the policing strategies put in practice during the direct racial contestation of the 1970s and early 1980s that expressed white intolerance at 'an official, institutional level'[156]. 'Black' was then used as a weapon by the white community as an expression of 'otherness' and excuse for separation. The 'Black Power' movement sought to remedy this, reclaiming 'black' from its negative connotations. Mercer explains

---

[152] Procter, 'Part One: 1948 to late 1960s', p.16
[153] Procter, 'Part One: 1948 to late 1960s', p.16
[154] Selvon, *The Lonely Londoners*, p.136
[155] Procter, 'Part One: 1948 to late 1960s', p.15
[156] James Procter, 'Part Two: late 1960s to mid-1980s', in *Writing Black Britain: 1948-1998*, ed. by J. Procter (Manchester: Manchester University Press, 2000), p.95

that it was at this moment that the black identity transcended beyond a 'biological or racial category [to become] a political signifier'[157]. This deliberate invocation of a collective identity 'rearticulated ['black'] as a sign of alliance and solidarity among... people sharing common historical experience'[158]. This led, in part, to the emergence of black British feminism in the 1970s, coupled with an increase in black women's writing. Vexed by their lack of representation, women writers such as Emecheta produced semi-autobiographical literature featuring admirable 'single-mother protagonists'[159] in desperate but deliberately *realistic* situations. The mounting repressions of their collective voice only increased determination to 'validate [their]... demonised... black British experience'[160] and accurately represent their history, culture and language.

In *Second-Class Citizen*, Emecheta shows the reader the grim reality of living as a Nigerian woman in 1960s London. Her protagonist, Adah experiences the violent shock of her own culture, history and language's dismissal as inferior and shameful. 'Black' becomes something she should have discarded upon entry into her beloved United Kingdom, a place that once represented her freedom. Upon arrival in London, Adah is informed by her husband Francis of their demotion to the 'low society'. Francis disregards her criticisms of their accommodation, informing her 'the only houses... black people with children... can get are horrors like these'[161], and that 'the day

---

[157] Kobena Mercer, *Welcome To The Jungle* (London: Routledge, 1987), p.11
[158] Mercer, *Welcome To The Jungle*, p.11
[159] Procter, 'Part Two: late 1960s to mid-1980s', p.97
[160] Procter, 'Part Two: late 1960s to mid-1980s', p.96

[she landed] in England [she became] a second-class citizen'[162]. She experiences the 'colour bar' in practice for herself when trying to find alternative housing, finding 'every door barred... even if they were willing to pay double the normal rent'[163]. After ignoring her husband and rebelling against the inferior position she has been assigned, Adah manages to secure a 'first-class job'[164] as a library assistant. She learns, though, that she is expected to give up her children to the care of a white foster-mother in order to work – a common practice amongst African housewives in England[165]. Only white women, it seemed, were allowed the privilege of keeping their children. Adah goes against this practice, and when her registered childminder, Trudy, neglects her duties in order to engage in prostitution, Adah reports her to the authorities. This negligent treatment results in her son, Vicky, contracting viral meningitis[166]. Adah is confident her descriptions of the children 'pulling rubbish out of the bin... [and washing] with [toilet] water'[167] will suffice to demonstrate Trudy's unsuitability. However, she is met by an unconcerned Children's Officer, overshadowed by a white woman adept at lying, and alienated by the unfamiliar laws and customs of this new society. Emecheta's post-dated interpretation of 1960s British racial intolerance is fiercer and more challenging than the

---

[161] Buchi Emecheta, *Second-Class Citizen* (Essex: Heinneman, 1994), p.35
[162] Emecheta, *Second-Class Citizen*, p.37
[163] Emecheta, *Second-Class Citizen*, p.71
[164] Emecheta, *Second-Class Citizen*, p.43
[165] Emecheta, *Second-Class Citizen*, p.44
[166] Emecheta, *Second-Class Citizen*, p.62
[167] Emecheta, *Second-Class Citizen*, p.51

account provided by Selvon in *The Lonely Londoners*. Because it was written during the bitter racial contestation of the 1970s, its revisitation of the past is unavoidably cynical, coloured by the knowledge of events to come and the desire to 'say it all'[168].

One notable difference is between the texts written by Selvon and Emecheta is the account of the assimilation undertaken by the black community during this period. Instead of the meek adaptation of culture and behaviour reported in *The Lonely Londoners*, *Second-Class Citizen*'s portrayal of men trying to incorporate two conflicting identities – 'black' and 'British' – is altogether more menacing. Her husband, Francis, undergoes an ugly transformation upon entry into Britain. When Adah reencounters him, Francis believes that he has become 'civilised'[169] in London, but in many ways has become a savage: laughing at death[170], committing adultery with white prostitutes[171], repeatedly disrespecting[172] and beating[173] his wife, and refusing to secure his family's financial security, now 'used to being worked for by a woman whom he knew belonged to him by right'[174]. The once-honoured aspects of his native culture are quickly abandoned – including the language, which he disallows his daughter Titi to speak[175] – and are only resorted to in order to

---

[168] Mercer, *Welcome to the Jungle*, pp.233-258
[169] Emecheta, *Second-Class Citizen*, p.34
[170] Emecheta, *Second-Class Citizen*, p.33
[171] Emecheta, *Second-Class Citizen*, p.63
[172] Emecheta, *Second-Class Citizen*, p.179
[173] Emecheta, *Second-Class Citizen*, p.154
[174] Emecheta, *Second-Class Citizen*, p.168
[175] Emecheta, *Second-Class Citizen*, p.53

humiliate his wife, Adah, in a communal ritual remnant of a court[176]. His self-image is frequently shifting, to the extent that even his religion changes to suit his mood and purpose. Emecheta's depiction of male aggression, domination, violence and sexuality (commonly engineered by Western influence) is common in the prose and poetry of this time, despite the fact these recurring themes tend of affirm the 'oppressive masculinities embodied within [negative] black identity formations of the 1970s'[177]. The inequality that exists between the 'black' and 'British' identities makes it difficult for a person to truly be both.

Gilroy's initial choice of words is poignant, then, considering the contrasting meanings of their origins. 'Nation' comes from 'nasci', meaning 'to be born'[178], whereas the Latin 'societas', from 'soctus', translates simply as 'companion'[179]. Are the collective black community condemned to this fate, too – allowed to sit alongside, but not permitted to be fully 'born into' the British nation? Gilroy believes there is still hope for a multiracial nation, as 'the complex pluralism of Britain's [current] inter-urban streets show that the elaborate syncretic processes [necessary] are underway [already]'[180]. Perhaps the Windrush's sixtieth anniversary could serve as a new symbolic beginning: one which initiates the universal recognition of

---

[176] Emecheta, *Second-Class Citizen*, pp.154-155
[177] Procter, 'Part Two: late 1960s to mid-1980s', p.96
[178] 'Nation', *The Compact Oxford English Dictionary for Students*, p.675
[179] 'Society', *The Compact Oxford English Dictionary for Students*, p.984
[180] Paul Gilroy, 'Cruciality and the Frog's Perspective: An Agenda of Difficulties for the Black Arts Movement in Britain', in *Writing Black Britain: 1948-1998*, ed. by J. Procter (Manchester: Manchester University Press, 2000), p.310

a proudly-multiracial Britain, awash with different races and cultures. A renewed embrace of a turbulent and difficult past could pave the way towards a future that promotes *equality* of societies: the beginning of a truly *United* Kingdom.

<u>Tearing Down the Binary</u>
(The Multiplicity of Hall's *Queer Theories)*

Hall's text provides a comprehensive catalogue of theories that strive to explain the process by which our sexual identities are constructed, developed and maintained. The complex and fractured relationship that these 'queer theories' have with one another – and the world which they examine – causes Hall to refer to them in the plural. The deviation from gender-specific theory into the much broader spectrum of 'queer' elevates the discussion to ontological heights, bringing the very question of 'being' into the debate. The fact that many of the concepts and ideas contained in *Queer Theories* originate from other areas of applied analysis (such as post-structuralism, postmodernism and philosophy) only serves to 'queer' the analytical process further. Instead of professing absolute truths, this text allows for active discussion of concepts, inviting both internal and external challenges to the ideas it contains from all academic fields.

The field of queer theory actively politicises the interaction between identity, sexuality and the assignment of social value to sexual desires. From the outset, Hall places sexual identity within the construct of our social existence in his text. He draws upon the ideas of Foucault and Lacan to place sexuality into the myriad of roles we assume throughout daily life, establishing the relationship between the social and the sexual elements of our selves. Far from defining us, Hall reinforces the idea that our sexual identities are 'artificial'[181] and confined by the social structure we exist within. He makes sure to draw attention to the oppressiveness of a concept of 'normality'. This is because the binary oppositions created within social environments tend to be weighted, creating a power differential between the dominant 'norm' and the marginal other. These conflicts may relate to differentials in gender (male/female), sexuality (heterosexual/homosexual) or judgements of morality (proper/improper). This suggests that even gender identity is, to a certain extent, socially constructed. Stryker notes that an 'epistemological rift [can occur] between gender signifiers and their signifieds'[182], indicating the separateness of our biological characteristics (our genitalia) and our understanding of how they impact on our sense of self (the assignment of masculine and feminine identities). Wittig reiterates this, arguing that terms such as 'man' or 'woman' are 'culturally overloaded'[183] with heterosexual connotations. By using such rigid 'hegemonic models of gender conformity'[184], areas such as female masculinity are either misunderstood (for example, labelled as 'inverted') or altogether ignored.

However, Hall is quick to point out Lacan's argument that 'phallocentric and heterocentric… entrenched [social] values are

---

[181] Donald E. Hall, *Queer Theories* (Hampshire: Palgrave Macmillan, 2003), p.2
[182] Susan Stryker, 'The Transgender Issue: An Introduction', *GLQ: A Journal of Lesbian and Gay Studies,* 4.2 (1998), p.147
[183] Monique Wittig, 'One Is Not Born a Woman', in *The Lesbian and Gay Studies Reader,* ed. by H. Abelove et al. (London: Routledge, 1993), pp.103-109
[184] Judith Halberstam, *Female Masculinity* (London: Duke University Press, 1998), p.9

potentially changeable, given their socially constructed status'[185]. Nietzsche, too, mounts a challenge against these 'contingent human constructs... [that] are in no way 'natural' or 'given''[186]. This is a significant point, as one of Hall's primary goals when creating this text was to demonstrate that these 'norms' can be challenged – the scientific system of separation and classification can, in turn, be closely examined. Queer theories, then, far from being restricted to the analysis of purely homosexual relations, can actively work to overturn the hetero/homo sexual binary. Instead of reinforcing misconceived stereotypes of effeminate gay men and 'butch' lesbians carrying the soul of the wrong sex inside them (which was Ulrichs' mutation of Plato's original concept of 'conjoined beings'[187]), this text explores ideas of 'performative' gender and sexuality, acknowledging 'the presence of both sexes... within oneself'[188] and throwing 'the reality of gender... into crisis'[189].

Hall is reluctant to resort to binary oppositions to explain the role of the 'queer' within society. Although he cites Halperin's concept of the 'queer' as 'whatever is at odds with the normal, the legitimate [and] the dominant'[190], he notes that this too is a simple inversion

---

[185] Hall, *Queer Theories*, p.62

[186] Dave Robinson, *Nietzsche and Postmodernism* (New York: Totem Books, 1999), pp.69-70

[187] Plato, *The Symposium* (Hammondsworth: Penguin, 1951)

[188] Hélèna Cixous, 'Sorties', in *The Newly Born Woman*, ed. by H. Cixous & C. Clement, trans. by B. Wing (Minneapolis: University of Minnesota Press, 1988), p.84

[189] Judith Butler, 'Introduction' in *Gender Trouble: Feminism and the Subversion of Identity* (London: Routledge, 1990), p. xxiii

[190] Dave Halperin, *Saint Foucault: Towards a Gay Hagiography* (Oxford: Oxford University Press, 1995), pp.61-2

and is therefore limited. He is more comfortable with Warner's disregard of the importance of homosexuality in queer theories, honouring instead a 'thorough resistance to regimes of the normal'[191] in constant abrasive flux and abandoning the fixed binary stance. It becomes clear throughout Hall's text that the most fundamental questions to be asked in the field of queer theorisation and critique address supposedly 'normal' states of being, alongside the many possibilities for 'abnormal being'[192]. Hall structuring his argument this way leads inevitably to an unavoidable rupture within ontological and philosophical thought – that is, the conflict between essentialist and constructionist/existentialist interpretations of our social and sexual existence. It is perhaps the most widely debated issue of all within both gender-specific and queer theorisation: is sexuality a preference or an orientation?

Both aspects of the nature/nurture argument contain their own potentially challenging connotations. Use of the word 'preference' denotes a chosen and changeable identity inside of conscious control. Those who consider homosexuality as a deviancy are able therefore to hold individuals morally culpable for their behaviour. However, assuming that identity has an enduring 'essence' or core reinforces the idea of a fixed binary map and ignores the anxious, confused and thoroughly unstable nature of sexuality[193]. It fails to

---

[191] Michael Warner, 'Introduction', in *Fear of a Queer Planet: Queer Politics and Social Theory,* ed. by M. Warner (Minneapolis: University of Minnesota Press, 1993), p. xxvi
[192] Hall, *Queer Theories*, p.56
[193] Julian Wolfreys, *Deconstruction·Derrida* (Basingstoke: Palgrave Macmillan,

disrupt the conformist Victorian notions of the normal and perverse, implying that homosexuality is distinct to only a small group of individuals rather than a characteristic fundamental to sexual development[194]. The implementation of this concept places the homosexual community firmly, and unfairly, in the minority.

It also disregards the 'morphic and multidirectional'[195] nature of desire, and its multiple possibilities for development, transgression and/or mutability. Hall cites examples of 'situational' or circumstantial homosexuality occurring in same-sex environments (such as prisons or boarding schools), and also self-identified homosexuals who have had previous orgasmic heterosexual experiences, to demonstrate this point. He even dares to touch upon issues of intergenerational desire and incest, a topic that only Rubin has considered to be 'legitimately within the thinkable realm of sexuality studies'[196]. Perhaps his most insightful contribution here, though, is to draw attention to the disproportionate importance placed upon interpersonal contact as the 'primary means by which we determine sexual identity, or delimit the forms of desire that identify us'[197], ignoring the solitary/masturbatory element of our sexual identity. The significance of intrapersonal sexual interaction

1998)
[194] Eve Sedgwick, *Epistemology of the Closet* (Berkley: University of California Press, 1990)
[195] Hall, *Queer Theories*, p.100
[196] Gayle Rubin, 'Thinking Sex: Notes for a Radical Theory of the Politics of Sexuality', in *The Lesbian and Gay Studies Reader*, ed. by H. Abelove et al. (London: Routledge, 1993), pp.3-44
[197] Hall, *Queer Theories*, p.110

cannot be underestimated. The explorative, self-searching nature of our sexual fantasies, coupled with the freedom and privacy they provide, allow for individuals to indulge in sexual transgressions they may not be comfortable physically performing (for example, heterosexual men fantasising about homosexual penetration; paedophilic or incestuous fantasies). Nevertheless, they still constitute part of our sexual identities.

Hall suggests that the marginal manifestations of our sexual desires are paramount to the understanding of desire itself, because it is through exploration of them we can recognise the social constructs we use to define and assign value to our everyday lives – an idea with clear poststructuralist connotations. His keenness to 'queer' these social constructs does not prevent him from acknowledging the fierce upheaval necessary required in doing so, though. To escape the binds and binaries of 'normality', societies must embrace the 'sharper degree of critical consciousness'[198] promoted by queer theorisation, using it to deconstruct previous historical or cultural understandings of what constitutes the self. This is a constant process, and one which can never be completed, given that every society is organic and in continuous fluctuation.

However, at no point does *Queer Theories* become defeatist. Throughout Hall's text there runs a consistent vein of hope – that unification and mutual understanding is, to a certain degree, possible, and that we may all progress to have a much more

---

[198] Hall, *Queer Theories*, p.176

thorough and accurate understanding of both ourselves and others. I personally plan to honour his concluding request, and shall respond to the call of "hey, queer!" with affirmation, positivity and – most of all – *pride*.

Interrupting Salih's *Migration to the North*
(Complications Arising from Bhabha's *Location of Culture)*

In Salih's text, *Migration to the North*[199], a newcomer to the unnamed narrator's Sudanese village – an Arab-African called Mustafe Sa'eed – relays details of one of his many sexual encounters with European women during his time in England. Mustafa's account unflinchingly describes his month-long endeavour to bed Isabella Seymour to its climactic end, wherein he attains the fulfilment of his selfish sexual desires without returning her declaration of love. This extract could easily be misread as a tale of straightforward sexual exploitation, in which the polarisations of 'Self' and 'Other' imposed by colonial discourse are inverted to allow Mustafa to assume a position of power. However, Bhabha demonstrates how such an oversimplification would be neither accurate nor desirable to the postcolonial critic.

Instead of striving for a reversal of value (assigning the coloniser the role of 'inferior' in the colonised's place), Bhabha complicates the standard critical approach of observing the total domination of one clearly-defined group by another. By overlooking the gaps and anxieties present for *both* participants in the colonial situation, one fails to fully appreciate the instability of colonial discourse's authority and the complexity of the relationship between the colonised and their colonisers. It is crucial to understand that neither group is fixed in a state of cultural 'purity': that is, *all* identities are

---

[199] Tayeb Salih, *Season of Migration to the North* (London: Heinemann, 1991)

fluctuating in a state of hybridity. Just as the postcolonial world cannot be polarised into 'good' (oppressed) and 'evil' (oppressors), the characters in Salih's text cannot be reduced to pure, fixed versions of 'European coloniser' (Isabella) and 'Arab-African colonised' (Mustafa). The way that Isabella is represented as both the 'white' European' and the 'bronze'[200] inheritor of a more exotic, imagined homeland ('Andalusia'[201]) shows how colonial concepts of inherent difference such as 'whiteness' are unstable. They rely on a rigid, fixed distinction between races which is impossible to maintain.

Mustafa's representation also shows how complex and antagonistic the process of hybridisation can be. Like the unnamed narrator, he has a Western education, but where the former enjoys elevated status in the Sudanese village, Mustafa struggles with the Western elements of his identity and finds himself in the 'liminal'[202] no-man's-land *between* cultures. Though Westernised in his mode of discourse, he assigns himself the alias of the exotic, 'pure' Arab-African Amin Hassan[203], compares himself to Othello[204] (Shakespeare's Moor) and repeatedly portrays his sexual desires as the embodied 'thirst'[205] of the 'southern... wilderness'[206]. It becomes

---

[200] Salih, *Season of Migration to the North* p.37
[201] Salih, *Season of Migration to the North,* p.42
[202] 'Liminality', in *Post-Colonial Studies: The Key Concepts*, ed. by B. Ashcroft, G. Griffins & H. Tiffin (London: Routledge, 2007 (second edition)), pp.117-118
[203] Salih, *Season of Migration to the North,* p.40
[204] Salih, *Season of Migration to the North,* p.38
[205] Salih, *Season of Migration to the North,* p.42
[206] Salih, *Season of Migration to the North,* p.38

apparent that both the 'European' (Isabella) and the 'Arab-African' (Mustafa) are unable to fix themselves to any one spatial or temporal location because of the 'tension [created] between the illusion of [their] padifference and the reality of [their] sameness'[207]. This tension is always present in the colonial situation, because of the inability to maintain a 'stable, final distinction between coloniser and colonised'[208]. Its absence leads to the development of underlying colonial anxiety. According to Bhabha, this anxiety opens a gap in colonial discourse that allows for the active 'agency'[209] of the colonised to emerge, providing an opportunity to exploit and undermine colonial power, thus allowing them to resist the dominance being exercised over them without resorting to the usual, violent form of opposition recognised by postcolonial theorists. One form that Bhabha focuses on is the circulation of colonial stereotypes, because it is a process in which both the coloniser and colonised participate. In this extract, Mustafa deliberately exploits and plays to 'anxiously repeated' colonial (mis)recognitions[210] in order to fulfil his sexual needs. By 'acceding to the [coloniser's] wildest fantasies'[211] in this way, Bhabha believed the colonised population are able to show the coloniser's position of mastery is

---

[207] David Huddart, *Homi K. Bhabha (Routledge Critical Thinkers)*, (London: Routledge, 2006), p.6
[208] Huddart, *Homi K. Bhabha*, p.6
[209] Homi K. Bhabha, 'The Postcolonial and the Postmodern: The Question of Agency', in *The Location of Culture* (London: Routledge, 2004), pp.245-282
[210] Homi K. Bhabha, 'The Other Question: Stereotype, Discrimination and the Discourse of Colonialism', in *The Location of Culture* (London: Routledge, 2004), p.95
[211] Homi K. Bhabha, 'Interrogating Identity: Frantz Fanon and the Postcolonial Prerogative', in *The Location of Culture* (London: Routledge, 2004), p.82

also a fantasy. Isabella also actively participates in the circulation of these colonial stereotypes and encourages Mustafa's enactment of the role of the 'Other'. The 'curiosity, gaiety [and] sympathy'[212] she feels when hearing his fabricated stories of 'streets [that] teemed with elephants, lions… and crocodiles'[213] inspires Mustafa to lie about how he 'lost [his] parents… to the Nile'[214]. Instead of feeling pity, Isabella is wrapped up in the exotic romanticism of Mustafa's tale – becoming '[en]snared [by] The Nile, that snake god'[215] – and her reaction is one of ecstasy. This corresponds to Bhabha's connection of the stereotype to Freudian notions of fetishism[216] on the grounds that it is 'predicated as much on mastery and pleasure as it is on anxiety and defence'[217]. Isabella is fulfilling her own selfish pleasure by 'affixing the unfamiliar to something… in a [repetitious] form which… vacillates between delight and fear'[218]. She cannot therefore be labelled as Mustafa's innocent victim.

Mustafa is fully aware that Isabella is attempting to objectify him. During intercourse, Mustafa describes how she 'gazed long and hard at [him], as though seeing… a symbol rather than reality'[219]. Under her gaze, he can feel himself being reduced to 'a naked, primitive creature [with] a spear… hunting elephants in the jungle'[220].

---

[212] Salih, *Season of Migration to the North*, p.38
[213] Salih, *Season of Migration to the North*, p.38
[214] Salih, *Season of Migration to the North*, pp.38-39
[215] Salih, *Season of Migration to the North*, p.39
[216] Sigmund Freud, 'Fetishism', in *On Sexuality, Vol VII* (Harmondsworth: Penguin Books, 1981), p.345
[217] Bhabha, 'Interrogating Identity…', pp.74-75
[218] Bhabha, 'Interrogating Identity…', p.73
[219] Salih, *Season of Migration to the North*, p.43

However, Isabella is not consciously aware (or unwilling to acknowledge) that her 'gaze' is being returned; that the process of objectification works both ways. Mustafa is objectifying Isabella too, adopting and adapting the techniques used within colonial discourse in a menacing form of mimicry. Salih creates an example of this when Mustafa describes 'pictur[ing] her obscenely naked as she said, "life is full of pain.'"[221]. The fact that he is more interested in 'the redness of her tongue... [than] the cloud of sadness that crossed her face'[222] resonates with the sexualised representations of exotic 'Eastern' women that swamp the colonial archives. There is also evidence of Mustafa seeing European woman as a territory to be 'taken' and conquered by an aggressor. In one sexually potent metaphor, Mustafa imagines 'driving [his] tent peg into [Isabella's] mountain summit'[223]. The parallel between sexual conquest and colonial invasion is drawn again when he compares his interaction with Isabella to 'the Arab soldiers' first meeting with Spain'[224] (when Andalusian territories fell under Moorish rule in 13th Century).

Though the postcolonial context of Salih's text should not be underestimated (as it clearly has implications on the modes of behaviour, thought and discourse used by the characters in this text), Bhabha would argue that the social effects of colonialism cannot be

---

[220] Salih, *Season of Migration to the North*, p.38
[221] Salih, *Season of Migration to the North*, pp.40-41
[222] Salih, *Season of Migration to the North*, p.40
[223] Salih, *Season of Migration to the North*, p.39
[224] Salih, *Season of Migration to the North*, p.42

reduced to predictable sets of generalised patterns: they are as 'multiple, polymorphous and perverse'[225] as the cultural structures that they exist within. Therefore, even his *own* terminology, though allowing for cultural complexities, cannot categorise the phenomena of mimicry and stereotyping with absolute certainty!

---

[225] Bhabha, 'Interrogating Identity...', p.67

Appropriated Bodies, Appropriated Voices
(The Silenced Women of the South African Transition)

South Africa was caught, towards the end of the twentieth century, in the fluctuations of a political and cultural transition. Though significant steps had been taken towards rectifying structures of social and economic exclusivity based on race – the most notable examples being the end of apartheid, and the implementation of interracial democratic elections in 1994 (which brought the ANC, and Mandela, to power) – the divisions created by racial hatred still resonated within the collective consciousness of South Africa. Narratives that focus specifically on interracial rape, such as Dangor's *Bitter Fruit*[226] and Coetzee's *Disgrace*[227], have thus been somewhat controversial. Many felt it was impossible to address the issue of sexual violence in South Africa without revisiting the interrelated racial hostilities[228]. It is clear that many would prefer 'silence [to be] drawn like a blanket… over the body of the [violated] woman'[229], supposedly in the name of racial reconciliation and progress.

However, I intend to demonstrate how certain patriarchal, political and discursive structures have perpetuated this cycle of female silence – and have thus allowed the differentiation of power between

---

[226] Achmat Dangor, *Bitter Fruit* (London: Atlantic Books, 2003)
[227] J.M. Coetzee, *Disgrace* (London: Vintage Books, 2000)
[228] South African Human Rights Commission (SAHRC), *Inquiry into Racism in the Media: Hearings Transcripts* XIV 3/3 (5th April 2000), p.125
[229] Coetzee, *Disgrace*, p.110

genders to continue post-apartheid – for much less selfless reasons. Furthermore, using Dangor's and Coetzee's texts as examples, I will discuss how even well-intentioned male representations of rape may still reinforce old concepts of conquest and dishonour – the use of which reduces women to objects of exchange, violated wombs and/or vessels for political messages.

Dangor's *Bitter Fruit* is set in late 1998 but addresses an act of violent rape committed 20 years earlier, in which the wife of an anti-apartheid activist – Lydia – is subjected to a brutal attack by a white security policeman named François Du Boise. This act is prompted by her husband Silas' involvement with the MK (the armed wing of the ANC). Though it is *her* body that is violated, she is neither the cause nor the intended recipient of Du Boise's aggression. The policeman appropriates Lydia's body so that he can use it to send 'a message of intimidation and humiliation addressed to her husband'[230]. Attacks of this kind were a frequent occurrence during apartheid. It was a method of demoralising members of the opposition in a society where the archaic male conception of rape as the usurpation of property still resonates. Warner notes that, in times of war, 'women's bodies become like letter boxes'[231], providing a medium of communication between male enemies. Therefore, in the process of being raped Lydia is being objectified: she becomes a possession

---

[230] Samuelson, 'Speaking Rape "Like A Man": Achmat Dangor's *Bitter Fruit*', p.2
[231] Marina Warner, quoted in 'Violence Against Women in Societies Under Stress' by Monica McWilliams, in *Rethinking Violence Against Women*, ed. by R.E. & R.P. Dobash (London: Sage, 1998), p.94

of her husband to be soiled and 'devaluated' by his white oppressor[232]. She is reduced to being damaged goods in an exclusively male power struggle; simultaneously denied both her subjectivity and her basic human rights. Rape, then, serves to lower a woman's status to 'the lowest strata [of the social hierarchy]'[233] – what Spivak referred to as 'subaltern'. This subjugated group are united by two defining factors: their oppressed status, and their inability to articulate their experiences. This is certainly relevant in terms of Lydia's character. In Silas' recollection of the event, the reader sees how she is robbed of speech as she is raped, and her voice is reduced to screams and moans[234]. Spivak argues that instead of trying to penetrate the veil of silence surrounding the subaltern class, emphasis should be placed on the underlying reasons why these individuals are unable to speak[235]. In Lydia's case, the decision to remain silent is rooted in a reluctance to engage with the etymologically-compromised terminology of rape. The only language available for her to remember and speak about her attack is a hegemonic discourse of patriarchal conquest, possession and dishonour. However, her husband's chance encounter with Du Boise in a local supermarket forces her to confront her traumatic past. For Silas, the night of Lydia's rape is an uncomfortable reminder of his *own* humiliation

---

[232] Rhonda Copelon, 'Surfacing Gender: Reconceptualising Crimes Against Women in Times of War', in *Violence Reader*, ed. by C. Besteman (New York: Palgrave Macmillan, 2002), p.203
[233233] Gayatri Chakravorty Spivak, 'Can the Subaltern Speak?', in *Colonial Discourse and Post-Colonial Theory: A Reader*, ed. by P. Williams & L. Chrisman (Hertfordshire: Harvester Wheatsheaf, 1994), p.78
[234] Dangor, *Bitter Fruit*, p.14
[235] Spivak, 'Can the Subaltern Speak?', pp.82-104

and as such, he requires her – as his dutiful wife – to share in his pain. Lydia responds to Silas' skewed perspective by using exclusively male concepts of shame and ownership against him: she goads him for allowing Du Boise steal his 'property', and tells him that his lack of a vengeful response proves that he isn't 'a real man'[236] Lydia is only able to engage in this method of speaking by physically changing the way her mouth feels. To speak 'like a man', she intentionally drinks her husband's 'sour', 'flat' beer[237]. For her, the fermented hops in the drink represent the 'breath' and 'taste' of *all* men[238], and this makes the first connection to the bitter fruit of the title. Being reduced to speaking in this brutal masculine discourse causes Lydia severe emotional distress. Samuelson argues that this language actually 'does violence to the women who [have to] speak it'[239], because it reinforces detrimental stereotypes of the female relationship with men. Its usage certainly contributes to Lydia's act of self-harm, in which she cuts open her feet using broken glass from Silas' beer bottle[240]. This is the only occasion that Lydia chooses to speak aloud about her rape. She shuns the opportunity to discuss her ordeal at both Du Boise's Truth & Reconciliation Commission amnesty hearing and with the medical professionals treating the wounds on her feet. Her injuries are thus explained as an 'accident' to doctors and family members[241], and her

---

[236] Dangor, *Bitter Fruit*, p.17
[237] *Ibid.*, pp.16-17
[238] *Ibid.*, pp.16-17
[239] Samuelson, 'Speaking Rape "Like A Man"…', p.2
[240] Dangor, *Bitter Fruit*, p.17
[241] *Ibid.*, p.19

private suffering continues unnoticed. Though the reader is given a candid account of the rape from Lydia's perspective, it is only made available through her son's uninvited intrusion into her diary entries. Both Mikey – and by default, the reader – become unwelcome spectators in a private memory of how Du Boise's thrusts were punctuated by Silas' fists hammering on the side of the police van[242]. In her subaltern state Lydia is unable to be authentically represented, so her experience is inevitably relayed via *male* perspectives – that of her husband, her son, and also Dangor (as a male author interpreting the feelings of a violated woman). The same is true of Lucy, Coetzee's primary female character in his alternative 'white victim' narrative *Disgrace,* published in 1999 (coinciding with Mbeki's election to power). In the course of Coetzee's text, Lucy – a white, middle-class lesbian living on her own farmland in the Eastern Cape – is gang-raped by three black African intruders[243]. Her rape is also related through the eyes of a male protagonist (and author), but in this case both are *white* men – a fact which enraged black members of the South African community, who believed the novel perpetuated negative stereotypes[244]. Lucy's father, David Lurie, provides the sole commentary for this event, despite the fact that he is locked in the bathroom in a semi-conscious state for the duration of her rape. The reader only experiences Lurie's imagined

---

[242] *Ibid.*, p.115
[243] Coetzee, *Disgrace*, pp.92-97
[244] Danielle Tran, ''*Swine!* The Word Still Rings in the Air': David's Reaction and the Perpetuation of Racial Conflict in J.M. Coetzee's *Disgrace*', postamble 7-1 (2011), p.1

projection of the rapist's actions, and Lucy is denied a voice with which to confirm or deny his portrayal. Though Lucy and Lydia differ in race, sexuality, and circumstances, they are united by their violation: the reason for their initiation into the subaltern class. These women have been 'muzzled' as a result of their sexual subjugation; the freedom of both their bodies and their voices compromised. Because of this, Lucy is similarly unable to speak to any male-dominated authorities in the aftermath of her ordeal. She feels able to inform the police about the robbery, the execution of her dogs and her father's assault, but omits details of her own attack. When officers arrive to inspect the scene of the crime, her bed has already been stripped and the evidence disposed of[245]. However, Lucy's silence is not simply 'an effort to forget or ignore the event, but rather… an attempt to remove herself from the racial politics behind the trauma'[246]. By speaking about the attack, she will inevitably confirm herself as the white victim of a black rapist. She believes that by doing so – and thus perpetuating old apartheid notions of 'black peril'[247] – she will reinforce the racial barriers that separate her from the surrounding black South African farming community. Though the attackers' motives are never confirmed, it becomes clear that both Lucy and her father suspect political motivations. As a white landowner and a lesbian in a country which largely expects women to operate under the constraints of hetero-

---

[245] Coetzee, *Disgrace*, p.109
[246] Tran, '…Perpetuation of Racial Conflict…', p.5
[247] Lucy Valerie Graham, 'Reading The Unspeakable: Rape in J.M. Coetzee's *Disgrace*', *Journal of South African Studies*, Vol.29 No.2 (June 2003), p.435

patriarchal practices like matrimony and male-controlled assets, Lucy feels that remaining on the farm 'without protection [makes her] fair game'[248]. Petrus – Lucy's black neighbour – offers her an 'alliance'[249], but his assistance comes at a heavy price: it depends on the surrender of her land, her agreement to become his third wife (despite her sexuality) and her continued silence regarding her attack. Lucy admits that she is prepared to suffer 'subjection [and] subjugation'[250] if it means no longer living in fear of sexual violation. David – from his male perspective – interprets Lucy's decision in strictly racial terms, believing that she seeks to 'expiate the crimes of the past by suffering in the present'[251]. This indicates that her silence is a form of self-imposed atonement for the past sins of her white ancestors. However, even if race *is* a consideration for Lucy, the fact that she must agree to such a proposal shows how 'women [in South Africa are still forced to] constantly negotiate their safety with men – those with whom they live, work and socialise, as well as those they have never met… – from a disadvantaged [gender] position'[252].

Both of the aforementioned texts show how problematic it can be for raped women to seek retribution for the wrongs they have suffered, or even find an appropriate method of articulation to convey their

---

[248] Coetzee, *Disgrace*, p.203
[249] *Ibid.*, p.203
[250] *Ibid.*, p.159
[251] *Ibid.*, p.112
[252] E. Stanko, *Everyday Violence* (London: Harper Collins, 1990), pp.85-86

painful experiences. However, failing to do so can have profound consequences. Their lack of narration creates a vacant space which is filled by unchallenged male voices. The male perspective often overlooks female suffering altogether and so makes the passive male's experience the primary focus. Even bodies such as the TRC, which were established specifically to acknowledge violations of human rights, admit that female reports of sexual violence are largely elided in favour of male narratives[253]. The disproportionate value placed upon male grievances fails to emphasise the need for female restoration, and can lead to acts of retaliatory violence committed by exclusively male consent. This is demonstrated in both *Disgrace* and *Bitter Fruit*, where the continuance of the violated women's silences allows male characters to appropriate the unclaimed status of 'victim' for themselves. David Lurie becomes increasingly preoccupied by his own feelings about Lucy's rape: his inability to prevent it, the corresponding guilt, and his desire to regain control of the situation. As a result, he begins to blur the boundaries that separate his and his daughter's suffering. His memory of their ordeal becomes one of shared experience: though his injuries are mostly cosmetic, Lurie describes 'a sense that… a vital organ… inside him… has [also] been used and abused'[254]. Furthermore, despite his daughter's requests that he 'only tell [people] what happened to [him]'[255] and respect her decision to remain silent, David continues see himself as the male figurehead of

[253] *Truth and Reconciliation Commission Final Report* (1998), Vol. 4.10 para 44
[254] Coetzee, *Disgrace*, p.107
[255] *Ibid.*, p.99

a wronged family, responsible for seeking retribution on both of their behalves. In fact, one could reasonably argue that the increasingly possessive language he uses in regards to Lucy is another form of objectification: she becomes akin to a precious item he has been entrusted to protect from danger. Lurie becomes fixated upon the race of Lucy's attackers and convinces himself that his daughter's integrity is threatened by *all* black South African men, whom '[he] associates [directly with] …crime, violence and brutality'[256]. Despite his previously amicable relationship with Petrus, in the aftermath of the intrusion Lurie suspects his involvement and questions him repeatedly, even before his relationship to Pollox is discovered. David's racial resentment is intensified by the discovery that his daughter has been impregnated by one of her rapists, and has chosen to nurture 'the worm [inside her] womb' rather than abort it[257]. His comparison of the baby's conception to being 'soiled [by a] dog's urine'[258] implies his belief of an animalistic, inherent savagery present in black men which could be passed on in the genes. This change in attitude is demonstrated through Lurie's sudden shift in language, which deviates from normal speech to a racialised vocabulary which strongly parallels the colonial discourse of the apartheid era. He begins to feel justified in using 'phrases that all his life he has avoided', and his need for retaliation becomes mixed with the specifically racial desire to 'teach [a black man] a lesson [and] *show*

---

[256] Tran, '…Perpetuation of Racial Conflict…', p.2
[257] Coetzee, *Disgrace*, p.199
[258] *Ibid.*, p.199

him his place '259. Therefore, when he catches Pollox spying on his naked daughter in the shower, he is compelled by 'elemental rage' to physically strike the boy[260]. Though this is portrayed as a protective father's act of revenge, Tran argues that by administering this violent beating Lurie reassumes the old position of 'white master'[261], perpetuating the same cycles of violence and racial hatred that his daughter is desperately trying to remove herself from. Graham goes further, arguing that Lurie has displaced his *own* undesirable traits onto the entire black male population in order to re-establish his sense of moral superiority. In the past, he too has exhibited sexually predatory behaviour (his 'not quite… rape' of Melanie Isaacs[262]) and similarly felt no need for remorse[263]. He thus recreates the old polarity between races, justifying it as the inherent difference that makes him *better*. This then allows him to portray his sexual subjugation of Melanie (as a white scholar) as motivated by Eros[264], whilst simultaneously maintaining his view of black men as uncontrollable savages. Turning Lucy's ordeal into his own personal battle for vengeance and redemption only serves to alienate his daughter. Lucy is furious that her father has appropriated her right to a reply (or lack thereof) and has decided to retaliate without her consent. She accuses him of denying her subjectivity, arguing that he perceives her as a minor character in his own life story[265]. The same

[259] *Ibid.*, p.206
[260] *Ibid.*, p206
[261] Tran, '…Perpetuation of Racial Conflict…', p.2
[262] Coetzee, *Disgrace*, p.25
[263] Graham, 'Reading The Unspeakable…', p.433
[264] Coetzee, *Disgrace*, p.52

is true for Lydia in *Bitter Fruit*, except that she must suffer this treatment from *both* men in her life. She, too, is reduced to a minor role and becomes the symbolic 'victim' in a story of rape appropriated by husband and son. Silas shows determination to make '[Lydia's] pain his tragedy'[266] in order to fuel his emasculated self-pity. He believes that his own traumatic experience of male torture – being made to 'tauza' and prove no items are concealed inside his anus[267] – is somehow comparable to the female experience of rape, and even expects sympathy from his wife for his suffering. Of course, it is *Lydia* who truly understands the burden of concealment: she has had to hide the uninvited penis, and the resulting memory of its intrusion, inside herself for twenty years. Silas' implication that her rape ordeal is not comparable to a male experience of torture therefore invokes her fury. Lydia refuses the gender division that Silas evokes, comparing the male penis to a 'torture instrument' and asserting that until he 'has been fucked up the arse against his will' their violation will never be comparable[268]. Lydia remains unaware of the second male appropriation of her suffering: that of her son, Mikey, whose discovery of his true heritage (as the 'bitter fruit' of rape) leads him to act in violent retaliation. He fixates upon the impurity of blood imposed upon him by the presence of the 'white father', and reasons that the only way to purge himself of his unwanted biological origins is to avenge his mother in Silas' place.

[265] *Ibid.*, p.198
[266] Dangor, *Bitter Fruit*, p.127
[267] *Ibid.*, p.17
[268] *Ibid.*, p18

However, this is not Mikey's only act of violent retribution. In his self-assigned role of judge and executioner, he also murders the incestuous father of his friend, Vinu. Despite her insistence that their sexual relationship was a thing of 'beaut[y]', Mikey imposes upon her his *male* diagnosis that she, too, is a victim of rape[269]. This implies a belief that the passive male's opinion has more relevance than the woman herself, and that it should be *he* who decides the course of retribution regardless of her feelings.

The victims of rape, then, are offered little opportunity for physical and emotional restoration. The atrocities they have had to suffer fuel male justifications for perpetuated cycles of violent retaliation. For the women trying to heal after these traumatic experiences, destructive male attempts to 'fight fire with fire' only serve to prolong, rather than alleviate, their suffering. However, their options for remedying their situation without male assistance are severely limited. At the close of *Disgrace*, Lucy feels her only choice is to surrender to the subjugation of the dominant male, Petrus, and agree to give up both her land and single status in exchange for protection. Dangor's Lydia chooses severance instead, deciding that she must separate from her husband in order to let go of the violent past. In an act of self-restoration, she engages in sexual relations with a young Mozambican, João, who is a guest at her husband's fiftieth birthday party and, in an inversion of her own objectification, uses his body as '[a] medium of expression' for her new-found sexual freedom[270].

---

[269] *Ibid.*, p.210

However, though Lydia's response may initially appear the more positive of the two, it is interesting to note that *both* women need a man to achieve their objective. Thankfully, Lucy and Lydia are fictional examples. However, there are countless South African women who have been forced to operate within political, patriarchal and discursive constraints, and thus further compromise themselves, for the sake of a cultural reconciliation. I firmly believe that reconciliation will not be possible until the victims of rape are given a forum – and a necessarily *female* language – with which to try and fill the silence themselves. Until *all* the voices of those hurt in the South African transition have been heard, the celebration of this new and unified nation remains premature.

---

[270] *Ibid.*, p.242

Bibliography

Essay 1:

Allen, Valerie, 'Medieval English, 500-1500', in *English Literature in Context*, ed. by Paul Poplawski (Cambridge: Cambridge University Press, 2008), pp. 1-97

Aristotle, translated by Butcher, S. H., *Poetics* (The Internet Classics Archive: Web Atomics, 1994) <http:classics.mit.edu//Aristotle/poetics.mb.txt>

Blake, William, *The Marriage of Heaven and Hell*, in *William Blake: The Complete Illuminated Books* (London: Thames & Hudson, 2000)

Bryson, Bill, 'The Plays', in *Shakespeare* (London: Harper Perennial, 2007), pp. 99-100

Croxford, L. 'The Uses of Interpretation in Hamlet', *Alif: Journal of Comparative Poetics*, 24 (2004), pp.93-120

de Grazia, Margaret, *Hamlet Without Hamlet* (Cambridge: Cambridge University Press, 2007)

Dillon, J. 'Is There A Performance In This Text?', *Shakespeare Quarterly*, 45 (1994), pp.74-87

Donaldson, P. 'Olivier, Hamlet and Freud', *Cinema Journal*, 26.4 (1987), pp.22-48

Heaney, Seamus, *Beowulf* (bilingual edition) (London: Faber and Faber, 2007)

Hiscock, Andrew, 'The Renaissance 1485-1660', in *English Literature in Context*, ed. by Paul Poplawski (Cambridge: Cambridge University Press, 2008), pp.110-207

Lawlor, J. J. 'The Tragic Conflict in *Hamlet*', *The Review of English Studies*, 1.2 (1950), pp.97-113

McManus, Barbara F., 'Outline of Aristotle's Theory of Tragedy in the Poetics', taken from *The College of New Rochelle Material* (Unknown: New York, 1999), pp. 1-4

Pope, Rob 'The Not-So-Strange Case of Shakespeare's Hamlet', in *The English Studies Book: An Introduction to Language, Literature and Culture* (second edition) (Oxon: Routledge, 2002), pp.78-81

Roach Jnr., J. R. 'Garrick, the Ghost and the Machine', *Theatre Journal*, 34.4 (1982), pp.431-440

Shakespeare, William, *Hamlet*, in *William Shakespeare: The Complete Works*, ed. by Stanley Wells and Gary Taylor (Oxford: Oxford University Press, 2005), pp. 681-718

Taylor, G. 'Hamlet', in *William Shakespeare: The Complete Works (second edition)*, ed. by Stanley Wells and Gary Taylor (Oxford: Oxford University Press, 2005), p. 681

Van Laan, T. F. 'Ironic Reversal in Hamlet', *Studies in English Literature*, 6.2 (1966), pp. 247-262

Werstine, P. 'The Textual Mystery of *Hamlet*', *Shakespeare Quarterly*, 39.1 (1988), pp.1-26

Young, Tory, 'Essays', in *Studying English Literature: A Practical Guide* (Cambridge: Cambridge University Press, 2008), pp. 79-118

Essay 2:

Academic Glossary of Literary Terms Online (Carson-Newham College, USA) <http://www.www.web.cn.edu/lit_terms.html>

Barry, Peter, *Beginning Theory: An Introduction to Literary and Cultural Theory* (third edition), (Manchester: Manchester University Press, 2009)

Bryson, Bill, *Shakespeare* (London: Harper Perennial, 2007)

Cuddon, J. A. (ed. by), *The Penguin Dictionary of Literary Terms & Literary Theory* (fourth edition), (London: Penguin Books, 1999)

Fenton, James, *An Introduction to English Poetry* (London: Penguin, 2003)

Goldberg, Natalie, *Writing Down The Bones: Freeing the Writer Within* (London: Shambhala, 2005)

Ferguson, M., Salter, J., & Stallworthy, J. (ed. by), *The Norton Anthology of Poetry* (fifth edition), (London: W. W. Norton & Company, 2005)

Leitch, V. B., Cain, W. E., Finke, L., & Johnson, B. (ed. by), *The Norton Anthology of Theory and Criticism* (first edition), (London: W. W. Norton & Company, 2001)

Online Etymology Dictionary <http://www.etymonline.com>

Oxford Concise English Dictionary <http://www.askoxford.com>

Paterson, Don (ed. by), *101 Sonnets* (London: Faber and Faber, 1999)

Petrarch, translated by Kline, A. S., *Canzoniere* (Poetry In Translation: 2002) <http://tkline.p.cc.net/PITBR/Italian/Petrarchhome.htm>

Pope, Rob, *The English Studies Book: An Introduction to Language, Literature and Culture* (Oxon: Routledge, 2002)

Poplawski, Paul (ed. by), *English Literature in Context'*, (Cambridge: Cambridge University Press, 2008)

Soanes, C., & Hawker, S. (ed. by), *The Compact English Dictionary for Students* (third edition), (Oxford: Oxford University Press, 2006)

Wells, Stanley, 'Sonnets and 'A Lover's Complaint'', in *William Shakespeare: The Complete Works* (second edition), ed. by Stanley Wells and Gary Taylor (Oxford: Oxford University Press, 2005), pp.777-798

Wells, S., & Orlin, L. C. (ed. by), *Shakespeare: An Oxford Guide*, (Oxford: Oxford University Press, 2003)

Wordsworth, W., & Coleridge, S. T., *Lyrical Ballads* (second edition), (London: Routledge Classics, 2005)

Wu, Duncan (ed. by), *Romanticism: An Anthology* (third edition), (Oxford: Blackwell Publishing, 2006)

Young, Tory, 'Essays' in *Studying English Literature: A Practical Guide* (Cambridge: Cambridge University Press, 2008), pp.79-118

Essay 3:

Aristotle, *Poetics* (unabridged), trans. by S. H. Butcher (New York: Dover Publications, 1997)

Aristotle, *Poetics*, in *The Norton Anthology of Theory and Criticism* (first edition), ed. by V. Leitch, E. Cain, L. FinPlato, *Republic*, trans. by R. Waterfield (Oxford: Oxford World Classics, 1993)

Cuddon, J.A. (ed. by), *The Penguin Dictionary of Literary Terms & Literary Theory* (London: Penguin, 1998)

Ferrari, G.R.F., 'Plato and Poetry', in in *The Cambridge History of Literary Criticism Volume I: Classical Criticism*, ed. by G.A. Kennedy (Cambridge: Cambridge University Press, 1997), pp.92-148

Leitch, Vincent B., 'Aristotle' in *The Norton Anthology of Theory and Criticism* (first edition), ed. by V. Leitch, E. Cain, L. Finke & B. Johnson (London: WW Norton & Co., 2001), pp. 86-90

Leitch, Vincent B., 'Plato' in *The Norton Anthology of Theory and Criticism* (first edition), ed. by V. Leitch, E. Cain, L. Finke & B. Johnson (London: WW Norton & Co., 2001), pp. 33-37

Leitch, Vincent B., 'Plotinus' in *The Norton Anthology of Theory and Criticism* (first edition), ed. by V. Leitch, E. Cain, L. Finke & B. Johnson (London: WW Norton & Co., 2001), pp.171-174

Halliwell, Stephen, 'Aristotle's *Poetics*', in in *The Cambridge History of Literary Criticism Volume I: Classical Criticism*, ed. by G.A. Kennedy (Cambridge: Cambridge University Press, 1997), pp.149-183

Herman, David (ed. by), *The Routledge Encyclopedia of Narrative Theory* (London: Routledge, 2008)

Lodge, David (ed. by), *Modern Criticism and Theory: A Reader* (London: Longman, 1988)

Nagy, Gregory, 'Early Greek Views of Poets and Poetry', in *The Cambridge History of Literary Criticism Volume I: Classical Criticism*, ed. by G.A. Kennedy (Cambridge: Cambridge University Press, 1997), pp.1-77

Plato, *Ion*, in *The Norton Anthology of Theory and Criticism* (first edition), ed. by V. Leitch, E. Cain, L. Finke & B. Johnson (London: WW Norton & Co., 2001), pp.37-49

Plato, *Republic*, in *The Norton Anthology of Theory and Criticism* (first edition), ed. by V. Leitch, E. Cain, L. Finke & B. Johnson (London: WW Norton & Co., 2001), pp.49-81

Plato, *Phaedrus*, in *The Norton Anthology of Theory and Criticism* (first edition), ed. by V. Leitch, E. Cain, L. Finke & B. Johnson (London: WW Norton & Co., 2001), pp.81-85

Plotinus, 'Eighth Tractate: On The Intellectual Beauty', in *The Norton Anthology of Theory and Criticism* (first edition), ed. by V. Leitch, E. Cain, L. Finke & B. Johnson (London: WW Norton & Co., 2001), pp.174-184

Selden, Raman (ed. by), *The Theory of Criticism, from Plato to the Present: A Reader* (Harlow: Pearson Education, 1988)

Essay 4:

Brennan, Timothy, 'Writing from Black Britain', *Literary Review,* 34 (Autumn 1990)

Constantine, Learie, 'Colour Bar', in *Writing Black Britain: 1948-1998*, ed. by J.Procter (Manchester: Manchester University Press, 2000), pp.63-68

Cuddon, J. A. (ed. by), *The Penguin Dictionary of Literary Terms & Literary Theory* (London: Penguin, 1998)

Emecheta, Buchi, *Second-Class Citizen* (Essex: Heinemann, 1994)

Fryer, Peter, *Staying Power: The History of Black People in Britain* (London: Pluto Press, 1984)

Getachew, Mahlete-Tsige, 'Marginalia: Black Literature and the Problem of Recognition', in *Write Black, Write British: From Post-Colonial to Black British Literature*, ed. by K. Sesay (Hertford: Hansib, 2005), pp.323-345

Gilroy, Paul, 'Blacks and Crime in Postwar Britain', in *Writing Black Britain: 1948-1998*, ed. by J. Procter (Manchester: Manchester University Press, 2000), pp.71-78

Gilroy, Paul, 'Cruciality and the Frog's Perspective: An Agenda of Difficulties for the Black Arts Movement in Britain', in *Writing Black Britain: 1948-1998*, ed. by J. Procter (Manchester: Manchester University Press, 2000), pp.307-320

Gilroy, Paul, *There Ain't No Black in the Union Jack – The Cultural Politics of Race and Nation* (London: Routledge, 1987)

Hall, S., Critcher, C., Jefferson, T., Clarke, J., & Roberts, B., *Policing the Crisis*, in *Writing Black Britain: 1948-1998*, ed. by J. Procter (Manchester: Manchester University Press, 2000), pp.170-177

Hall, Stuart, 'Racism and Reaction', in *Five Views of Multi-Cultural Britain* (London: Commission for Racial Equality, 1978)

Hall, Stuart, 'Reconstruction Work: Images of Postwar Black Settlement', in *Writing Black Britain: 1948-1998*, ed. by J. Procter (Manchester: Manchester University Press, 2000), pp.82-94

Innes, C. L., *A History of Black and Asian Writing in Britain* (second edition), (Cambridge: Cambridge University Press, 2008)

Macczynska, Magdalena, 'The Aesthetics of Realism in Contemporary Black London Fiction', in *'Black' British Aesthetics Today*, ed. by R. V. Arana (Newcastle upon Tyne, 2009), pp.135-149

Mercer, Kobena, '"Diaspora Didn't Happen in a Day': Reflections on Aesthetics and Time', in *'Black' British Aesthetics Today*, ed. by R. V. Arana (Newcastle upon Tyne, 2009), pp.66-78

Mercer, Kobena, *Welcome to the Jungle* (London: Routledge, 1987)

Nasta, Susheila, 'Crossing Over and Shifting the Shapes: Sam Selvon's Londoners', in *Home Truths: Fictions of the South Asian Diaspora in Britain* (Hampshire: Palgrave, 2002), pp.56-92

Procter, James, *Dwelling Places: Postwar Black British Writing* (Manchester: Manchester University Press, 2003)

Procter, James (ed. by), *Writing Black Britain: 1948-1998* (Manchester: Manchester University Press, 2000), pp.1-12, 13-16 & 95-97

Selvon, Sam, *The Lonely Londoners* (London: Penguin Books, 2006)

Soanes, Catherine (ed. by), *The Compact Oxford English Dictionary for Students* (third edition), (Oxford: Oxford University Press, 2006)

Stein, Mark, *Black British Literature: Novels of Transformation* (Ohio: The Ohio State University Press, 2004)

SuAndi, 'Cultural Memory and Today's Black British Poets and Live Artists', in *'Black' British Aesthetics Today*, ed. by R. V. Arana (Newcastle upon Tyne, 2009), pp.31-49

Essay 5:

Butler, Judith, *Gender Trouble: Feminism and the Subversion of Identity* (London: Routledge, 1990)

Cixous, Hélèna, 'Sorties', in *The Newly Born Woman*, ed. by H. Cixous & C. Clement, trans. by B. Wing (Minneapolis: University of Minnesota Press, 1988)

Halberstam, Judith, *Female Masculinity* (London: Duke University Press, 1998)

Hall, Donald E., *Queer Theories* (Hampshire: Palgrave Macmillan, 2003)

Halperin, Dave, *Saint Foucault: Towards a Gay Hagiography* (Oxford: Oxford University Press, 1995)

Plato, *The Symposium* (Hammondsworth: Penguin, 1951)

Robinson, Dave, *Nietzsche and Postmodernism* (New York: Totem Books, 1999)

Rubin, Gayle, 'Thinking Sex: Notes for a Radical Theory of the Politics of Sexuality', in *The Lesbian and Gay Studies Reader*, ed. by H. Abelove et al. (London: Routledge, 1993)

Sedgwick, Eve, *Epistemology of the Closet* (Berkley: University of California Press, 1990)

Stryker, Susan, 'The Transgender Issue: An Introduction', in *GLQ: A Journal of Lesbian and Gay Studies,* 4.2 (1998)

Warner, Michael, 'Introduction', in *Fear of a Queer Planet: Queer Politics and Social Theory,* ed. by M. Warner (Minneapolis: University of Minnesota Press, 1993)

Wittig, Monique, 'One Is Not Born a Woman', in *The Lesbian and Gay Studies Reader*, ed. by H. Abelove et al. (London: Routledge, 1993), pp.124-169

Wolfreys, Julian, *Deconstruction·Derrida* (Basingstoke: Palgrave Macmillan, 1998)

Essay 6:

Ashcroft, Bill, Helen Tiffin & Gary Griffin (ed. by), 'Ambivalence', in *Post-colonial Studies: The Key Concepts* (London: Routledge, 2007 (second edition)), pp.10-11

Ashcroft, Bill, Helen Tiffin & Gary Griffin (ed. by), 'Agency', in *Post-colonial Studies: The Key Concepts* (London: Routledge, 2007 (second edition)), pp.6-7

Ashcroft, Bill, Helen Tiffin & Gary Griffin (ed. by), 'Colonial Desire', in *Post-colonial Studies: The Key Concepts* (London: Routledge, 2007 (second edition)), p.36

Ashcroft, Bill, Helen Tiffin & Gary Griffin (ed. by), 'Colonial Discourse', in *Post-colonial Studies: The Key Concepts* (London: Routledge, 2007 (second edition)), pp.36-38

Ashcroft, Bill, Helen Tiffin & Gary Griffin (ed. by), 'Hybridity' in *Post-colonial Studies: The Key Concepts* (London: Routledge, 2007 (second edition)), pp.108-111

Ashcroft, Bill, Helen Tiffin & Gary Griffin (ed. by), 'Liminality', in *Post-colonial Studies: The Key Concepts* (London: Routledge, 2007 (second edition)), pp.117-118

Ashcroft, Bill, Helen Tiffin & Gary Griffin (ed. by), 'Mimicry', in *Post-colonial Studies: The Key Concepts* (London: Routledge, 2007 (second edition)), pp.124-127

Ashcroft, Bill, Helen Tiffin & Gary Griffin (ed. by), 'Other, & Othering', in *Post-colonial Studies: The Key Concepts* (London: Routledge, 2007 (second edition)), pp.154-158

Bhabha, Homi K., 'Interrogating Identity: Frantz Fanon and the Postcolonial Prerogative', in *The Location of Culture* (London: Routledge, 2004), pp.57-93

Bhabha, Homi K., 'Of Mimicry and Man: The Ambivalence of Colonial Discourse', in *The Location of Culture* (London: Routledge, 2004), pp.121-131

Bhabha, Homi K., 'The Other Question: Stereotype, Discrimination and the Discourse of Colonialism', in *The Location of Culture* (London: Routledge, 2004), pp.94-120

Bhabha, Homi K., 'Signs Taken for Wonders Questions of Ambivalence and Authority under a Tree outside Delhi, May 1817', in *The Location of Culture* (London: Routledge, 2004), pp.145-174

Bhabha, Homi K., 'Sly Civility', in *The Location of Culture* (London: Routledge, 2004), pp.132-144

Freud, Sigmund, 'Fetishism', in *On Sexuality, Vol VII* (Harmondsworth: Penguin Books, 1981), pp.340-375

Huddart, David, *Homi K. Bhabha* (London: Routledge, 2006), pp.1-170

Young, Robert J. C., 'Colonialism and the Desiring Machine', in *Colonial Desire: Hybridity in Theory, Culture and Race* (London: Routledge, 1995), pp.159-182

Salih, Tayeb, *Season of Migration to the North* (London: Heinemann, 1991), pp.36-44

Young, Robert J. C., 'Culture and the History of Difference', in *Colonial Desire: Hybridity in Theory, Culture and Race* (London: Routledge, 1995), pp.29-54

Young, Robert J. C., 'Hybridity and Diaspora', in *Colonial Desire: Hybridity in Theory, Culture and Race* (London: Routledge, 1995), pp.1-28

Essay 7:

Ashcroft, Bill, Helen Tiffin & Gary Griffin (ed. by), 'Ambivalence', in *Post-colonial Studies: The Key Concepts* (London: Routledge, 2007 (second edition)), pp.10-11

Ashcroft, Bill, Helen Tiffin & Gary Griffin (ed. by), 'Agency', in *Post-colonial Studies: The Key Concepts* (London: Routledge, 2007 (second edition)), pp.6-7

Ashcroft, Bill, Helen Tiffin & Gary Griffin (ed. by), 'Colonial Desire', in *Post-colonial Studies: The Key Concepts* (London: Routledge, 2007 (second edition)), p.36

Ashcroft, Bill, Helen Tiffin & Gary Griffin (ed. by), 'Colonial Discourse', in *Post-colonial Studies: The Key Concepts* (London: Routledge, 2007 (second edition)), pp.36-38

Ashcroft, Bill, Helen Tiffin & Gary Griffin (ed. by), 'Hybridity' in *Post-colonial Studies: The Key Concepts* (London: Routledge, 2007 (second edition)), pp.108-111

Ashcroft, Bill, Helen Tiffin & Gary Griffin (ed. by), 'Liminality', in *Post-colonial Studies: The Key Concepts* (London: Routledge, 2007 (second edition)), pp.117-118

Ashcroft, Bill, Helen Tiffin & Gary Griffin (ed. by), 'Mimicry', in *Post-colonial Studies: The Key Concepts* (London: Routledge, 2007 (second edition)), pp.124-127

Ashcroft, Bill, Helen Tiffin & Gary Griffin (ed. by), 'Other, & Othering', in *Post-colonial Studies: The Key Concepts* (London: Routledge, 2007 (second edition)), pp.154-158

Bhabha, Homi K., 'Interrogating Identity: Frantz Fanon and the Postcolonial Prerogative', in *The Location of Culture* (London: Routledge, 2004), pp.57-93

Bhabha, Homi K., 'Of Mimicry and Man: The Ambivalence of Colonial Discourse', in *The Location of Culture* (London: Routledge, 2004), pp.121-131

Bhabha, Homi K., 'The Other Question: Stereotype, Discrimination and the Discourse of Colonialism', in *The Location of Culture* (London: Routledge, 2004), pp.94-120

Bhabha, Homi K., 'Signs Taken for Wonders Questions of Ambivalence and Authority under a Tree outside Delhi, May 1817', in *The Location of Culture* (London: Routledge, 2004), pp.145-174

Bhabha, Homi K., 'Sly Civility', in *The Location of Culture* (London: Routledge, 2004), pp.132-144

Freud, Sigmund, 'Fetishism', in *On Sexuality, Vol VII* (Harmondsworth: Penguin Books, 1981), pp.340-375

Huddart, David, *Homi K. Bhabha* (London: Routledge, 2006), pp.1-170

Salih, Tayeb, *Season of Migration to the North* (London: Heinemann, 1991), pp.36-44

Young, Robert J. C., 'Colonialism and the Desiring Machine', in *Colonial Desire: Hybridity in Theory, Culture and Race* (London: Routledge, 1995), pp.159-182

Young, Robert J. C., 'Culture and the History of Difference', in *Colonial Desire: Hybridity in Theory, Culture and Race* (London: Routledge, 1995), pp.29-54

Young, Robert J. C., 'Hybridity and Diaspora', in *Colonial Desire: Hybridity in Theory, Culture and Race* (London: Routledge, 1995), pp.1-28

About Joanne Weselby

Joanne M. Weselby (1985-) was born in Sutton in Ashfield, England and grew up a stone's throw from Sherwood Forest.

As an adult, she went on to obtain a first class BA (Hons) in English Literature and Creative Writing from Nottingham Trent University in 2012, and was awarded both the Five Leaves Prize and the Pat McLernon Prize for outstanding academic achievements in her chosen field.

She now works freelance as a writer, academic researcher and copyeditor.

Books by Joanne M. Weselby

- ❖ 'First Class English Essays: A Collection of Short Essays'

- ❖ 'Citations Made Simple: A Guide to Easy Referencing'

- ❖ 'Never Too Late: A Mature Student's Guide to Going to University'

Success Stories?

If, after reading this book, you've found it to be helpful, why not let myself and others know about it by posting a review?

Alternatively, visit my Fan Page on Facebook at:
https://www.facebook.com/jmweselby

Like, share, and/or leave me a comment – I'd be delighted to hear from you!

Printed in Great Britain
by Amazon